Armies of the Italian Wars of Unification 1848–70 (2)

Papal States, Minor States & Volunteers

Gabriele Esposito • Illustrated by Giuseppe Rava

Series editor Martin Windrow

OSPREY

Bloomsbury Publishing Plc

PO Box 883, Oxford, OX1 9PL, UK

1385 Broadway, 5th Floor, New York, NY 10018, USA

E-mail: info@ospreypublishing.com

www.ospreypublishing.com

OSPREY is a trademark of Osprey Publishing Ltd

First published in Great Britain in 2018

A catalogue record for this book is available from the British Library

ISBN: PB 9781472826244; eBook 9781472826220; ePDF 9781472826213; XML 9781472826237

18 19 20 21 22   10 9 8 7 6 5 4 3 2 1

Editor: Martin Windrow
Map by JB Illustrations
Index by Alan Rutter
Typeset by PDQ Digital Media Solutions, Bungay, UK
Printed in China through World Print Ltd.

Osprey Publishing supports the Woodland Trust, the UK's leading woodland conservation charity. Between 2014 and 2018 our donations are being spent on their Centenary Woods project in the UK.

To find out more about our authors and books, visit **www.ospreypublishing.com**. Here you will find extracts, author interviews, details of forthcoming events and the option to sign up for our newsletter.

Dedication

To my parents Maria Rosaria and Benedetto, who always support my dreams with love and intelligence.
This book is also dedicated to the memory of all the young Italian volunteers who gave their lives for the unification of my country.

Editor's Note

For reasons of space, it has not been possible to divide these two connected Men-at-Arms titles devoted to the armies of the three Italian Wars of Unification (1848–49, 1859 & 1866–70 – collectively known as the *Risorgimento*) into exactly consistent geographical and chronological halves.
The first book, MAA 512, covers the organization of the two largest armies – those of Piedmont (the Kingdom of Sardinia, ruled by the Royal House of Savoy) and of the Kingdom of the Two Sicilies (ruled by the Bourbon monarchy of Naples) – throughout the whole period. It also includes a **Chronology of the First War, 1848–49.** Readers will find it useful to study the present volume in conjunction with MAA 512.

Acknowledgements

Thanks are due to the series editor Martin Windrow, for his support and encouragement from the beginning of this project. Another special acknowledgement goes to Giuseppe Rava, for his magnificent plates; his vivid use of colour and his genius in composition have reconstructed the uniforms of the *Risorgimento* in their original splendour.
Most of the pictures published in this book were obtained from the Digital Collections of the New York Public Library, or (where so credited) from the Anne S.K. Brown Military Collection at Brown University Library, Providence RI, USA. The original files are available at:
https://digitalcollections.nypl.org/
https://repository.library.brown.edu/studio/collections/id_619/

Artist's Note

Readers may care to note that the original paintings from which the colour plates in this book were prepared are available for private sale. All reproduction copyright whatsoever is retained by the publisher. All enquiries should be addressed to:

Giuseppe Rava, via Borgotto 17, 48018 Faenza (RA), Italy
info@g-rava.it

The publishers regret that they can enter into no correspondence upon this matter.

OPPOSITE
Infantrymen of the *Brigata Sacchi,* of volunteer reinforcements sent to Garibaldi in Sicily by the Piedmontese government in July 1860. (Left) Dark blue kepi with red bottom band and piping and brass buglehorn badge; grey greatcoat with a white rank stripe on the forearms; white trousers, spat-gaiters and waistbelt (note the Savoy cross on the brass plate) and black shoes. (Right) The same kepi and legwear, with an all-white jacket; visible under this is a red shirt, which has a green front placket strip. (Courtesy Anne S.K. Brown Military Collection, Brown University Library, Providence RI)

ARMIES OF THE ITALIAN WARS OF UNIFICATION 1848-70 (2)

PAPAL STATES, MINOR STATES & VOLUNTEERS

INTRODUCTION

Even in summary, the history of the many regional armies that took part in the various stages of the *Rigorgimento* over 22 years is unavoidably complex, and readers are invited to study both this book and Men-at-Arms 512 together (see Editor's Note opposite).

The historical and political background to Italy's long struggle for independence from Austria, internal strife, and eventual unification has been outlined in the first of these two books, Men-at-Arms 512. That volume includes a Chronology of the First War of Unification (1848–49), but describes the pre-unification armies of both Piedmont and the Kingdom of the Two Sicilies throughout the whole period, as well as the unified Italian Army of the 1860s, for which that of Piedmont formed the nucleus.[1]

This second book includes a Chronology of the Second and Third Wars, but is otherwise devoted to the pre-unification armies of the Papal States, Grand Duchy of Tuscany, Duchy of Modena and Duchy of Parma throughout the *Risorgimento*, and to the short-lived revolutionary armies formed during 1848–49. A certain degree of overlap is unavoidable, and the forces of the 1859–60 Central Italian League also mentioned here have already been described in MAA 512 with regard to their later absorption by the army of Piedmont.

Finally, this second book covers the various corps of volunteers that were active during the entire period. After the harsh lessons of the First War, later patriot volunteers began to assemble around the charismatic figure of Giuseppe Garibaldi. The practice of forming many small units was abandoned in favour of larger and more organized corps, starting from 1859 with the creation of the *Cacciatori delle Alpi*. In 1860 Garibaldi repeated this process with his famous *Camicie Rosse* ('Red Shirts'), who gradually evolved into a genuine army some 25,000 strong. In 1866 the newly unified Kingdom of Italy created a central corps of volunteers, the *Corpo Volontari Italiani*, again under the command of Garibaldi.

---

1   For simplicity, throughout this text the political entity ruled by King Victor Emmanuel II of the Royal House of Savoy will be called Piedmont rather than the Kingdom of Sardinia, to avoid confusion with the actual island of Sardinia. Thus, we refer to the *Armata Sarda* as the Piedmontese Army. Also note that some personal names have been Anglicized.

CHRONOLOGY: SECOND & THIRD WARS OF UNIFICATION, 1855–70

April 1855–March 1856 Piedmontese military involvement in Crimean War, with main aim of gaining favour with French Emperor Napoleon III, thus laying foundation for military alliance in anticipation of renewed conflict with Austria in northern Italy. Piedmont's participation earns it a place at the Paris peace conference, where King Victor Emmanuel's Prime Minister Cavour promotes cause of Italian unification to the major European powers.

21 April 1858 Plombières Agreement between Napoleon III and Cavour. In exchange for future military help, Piedmont would have ceded Savoy and Nice to France; in the event, these severe sacrifices were never demanded.

1859:
January Signature of official Franco-Piedmontese treaty, which commits France to intervene alongside Piedmont in the event of Austrian military aggression.

9 March–29 April Cavour deliberately provokes Vienna with a series of aggressive military manoeuvres close to the border with Austrian-ruled Lombardy. Austria issues ultimatum **(23 April)**, demanding complete demobilization of Piedmontese Army. Its rejection leads to **outbreak of Second War of Unification (29 April)**.

20 May First action of the war at Montebello. Despite a numerical advantage, Gen Stadion's Austrian V Corps units, unwisely dispersed, are defeated by Gen Forey's Div of French I Corps plus Piedmontese troops.

All five Piedmontese divisions then manoeuvre against the Austrian right while the French army advances north across River Po, to swing east on the Austrian army's northern flank.

30–31 May Battle of Palestro: Piedmontese cross Sesia R. and 2nd–4th Divs capture fortified villages, holding them against counter-attack. Faced by French turning movement around his right, Austrian commander Gyulai then retreats east behind Ticino R. into defensive positions before Milan.

4 June Battle of Magenta: French II Corps and Imperial Guard defeat Austrian I & II Corps, opening road to Milan, which is occupied by Franco-Piedmontese troops four days later.

24 June Simultaneous battles of San Martino and Solferino. At Solferino, 80,000 French and 13,000 Piedmontese decisively defeat 100,000 Austrians, and at San Martino 22,000 Piedmontese drive 20,000 Austrians into retreat. Both sides suffer heavy losses – c. 17,000 allied casualties to 22,000 Austrian.

11–12 July Armistice of Villafranca concludes Second War of Unification. Piedmont annexes Lombardy, but the Italians are not satisfied by the peace terms, since they had also hoped to occupy Venice and its surrounding territory.

1860:
11–12 March To compensate for not receiving Venice, Cavour institutes plebiscites on annexation to Piedmont of Central Italian League territories (Duchies of Modena and Parma, Papal Legations of Romagna, and Grand Duchy of Tuscany). Majority of populations vote enthusiastically in favour, and annexation to Victor Emmanuel's kingdom becomes effective after a matter of days.

5 May Garibaldi's 'Expedition of the Thousand' leaves Quarto, near Genoa. Six days later, these 'Red Shirt' volunteers disembark at Marsala in Sicily, to begin the liberation of the South from the Bourbon-ruled Kingdom of the Two Sicilies.

15 May Garibaldi's success in clash at Calatafimi increases local recruitment and lowers Neapolitan morale.

30 May Backed by widespread popular rising, the Red Shirts occupy the Sicilian capital, Palermo.

17–24 July Battle of Milazzo near Messina; fall of last Bourbon stronghold in Sicily.

19 August Garibaldi's force lands in mainland Italy, meeting little resistance as the Bourbon army quickly collapses.

7 September The Red Shirts enter Naples, capital of the Kingdom of the Two Sicilies.

18 September Piedmontese forces totalling 39,000, invading Papal territories in east-central Italy, defeat 10,000 Papal troops at Castelfidardo near Ancona. Only Rome and immediate surroundings remain in Papal hands, thanks to French military protection (since Napoleon III needs the domestic support of the Catholic Church).

26 September–2 October Decisive battle of the Volturno R. between the Bourbon army and Garibaldi's Red Shirts; in a failed attempt to break Garibaldi's lines and recapture Naples, 30,000 Neapolitan regulars are defeated by 25,000 volunteers. The Bourbon King Francis II retreats with all his remaining forces to their last bastion, Gaeta.

20 October Victor Emmanuel II and his Piedmontese army join forces with Garibaldi's 'Army of the South' at Teano.

5 November Piedmontese army begins siege of Gaeta.

1861:
13 February Gaeta finally surrenders; King Francis II goes into exile in Rome, under protection of the Pope.

17 March Proclamation of the Kingdom of Italy, under King Victor Emmanuel II.

29 August 1862 Marching on Rome in defiance of Italian government policy, Garibaldi and his Red Shirts are defeated by Italian Army regulars in the Aspromonte mountains of Calabria, and Garibaldi is temporarily placed under arrest. The new kingdom's relationships with Rome and Venice remain unresolved.

1866:
8 April Signing of treaty of alliance between Prussia and Kingdom of Italy, the latter taking advantage of rising tensions between Prussia and Austria.

14 June Outbreak of Austro-Prussian War.

20 June Outbreak of Third War of Unification.

24 June Disastrous Italian defeat at battle of Custoza; 120,000 troops of newly unified Italian Army are defeated by 75,000 Austrians.

3 July Decisive Prussian victory over Austria at battle of Sadowa (Königgratz).

20 July Italian defeat in naval action of Lissa, between Italian fleet (Adm Persano) and much smaller Austrian force (Adm Tegetthoff).

12 August Conclusion of Third War of Unification by Armistice of Cormons between Italy and Austria.

23 August Austro-Prussian War ends in complete victory for Prussia.

3 October Signing of Treaty of Vienna, under terms of which Austria is forced to cede Venice despite having defeated the Italians decisively at Custoza and Lissa.

3 November 1867 Battle of Mentana, between Garibaldi's Red Shirts and the Papal Army supported by a small French expeditionary corps. Garibaldi's second attempt to invade Rome without Italian government support is again defeated.

19 July 1870 Outbreak of Franco-Prussian War enables Italy to plan invasion of last Papal territories without French interference.

20 September 1870 Occupation of Rome by Italian Army, after brief and purely symbolic defence by the Papal military forces.

Italian Unification is complete.

Map showing the Italian states in 1847, including the Duchy of Lucca (which was annexed by Tuscany in that year).

Most of the important battles of the *Risorgimento* were fought near major cities:

First War (1848–49): Goito (north of Mantua); Peschiera (west of Verona); Pastrengo (north-west of Verona); Vicenza (west-north-west of Venice); Cornuda (north-west of Venice); Custoza (south-west of Verona); Bologna; Messina (Sicily); Novara (west of Milan); Brescia; Genoa; Palermo (Sicily); Livorno; Ancona; Rome; Venice.

Second War (1859–61): Magenta (west of Milan); Solferino (north of Mantua); Calatafimi (north-east of Marsala, Sicily); Castelfidado, south-east of Ancona; Volturno River (north of Naples); Gaeta.

Third War (1866): Custoza (south-west of Verona); Lissa Island (off Dalmatian coast).

(Map by JB Illustrations)

THE PAPAL ARMY, 1848–70

See Plate A for information on uniforms of the Papal States forces in 1848–49.

This lieutenant serves in the Squadron of Light Cavalrymen formed on 30 May 1859 from former Austrian Army cavalry veterans, and disbanded on 10 October 1860, when its troopers were absorbed into the Dragoon Regiment's new foreign 2nd Squadron. Colours: dark green shako with yellow top band, piping, pompon and falling plume, white lace loop, tricolour national cockade, gilt buglehorn. Dark green jacket with yellow collar, pointed cuffs and frontal piping; white epaulette and contre-epaulette. White-and-yellow pouch belt with gilt picker fittings; white sword belt, black sword knot with gold tassel. Grey trousers with yellow double side-stripes. Dark green shabraque with yellow border and buglehorn.

The Papal Army, previously a small internal security force, would become the third largest in Italy after those of Piedmont and Naples (the Two Sicilies). In 1847–48, Pius IX permitted the creation of a *Guardia Civica* (National Guard), and during the First War public pressure obliged him to send troops against the Austrians. After the brief revolutionary Roman Republic (9 February–2 July 1849) France left an occupation force in the Papal States, whose authorities took until 1852 to reorganize their own forces.

In 1859, however, when France sided with Piedmont, the territories known as 'Papal Legations' were lost. Under the threat of Piedmontese invasion, with the prospect that the French garrison would adopt a neutral position, the Papal authorities had to strengthen their forces urgently. This was achieved under the experienced French Gen Lamoricière as army commander, and a priestly Belgian veteran of the Foreign Legion, Monseigneur de Merode, as minister of war. A widely publicized religious appeal (for what even became known as 'the Ninth Crusade') attracted many volunteers – mostly from France, Belgium, Ireland and Austria – who brought a new enthusiasm into the Papal forces.

After the defeat at Castelfidardo in September 1860 the Pope had to cede much of his territory to Piedmont and to reduce his army, disbanding most of the new foreign units. France agreed with Italy to withdraw its force from Rome in 1866, but returned the following year in order to stop the advance of Garibaldi's Red Shirts. In 1870, with France desperately defending itself against Prussia, the way was clear for the Italians to enter Rome.

ORGANIZATION:

National infantry[2]

In 1847 the army included three regiments of national infantry: one each of grenadiers, fusiliers and light *cacciatori* (chasseurs). Each had 2 battalions of 8 companies (6 centre and 2 'flank' – i.e. grenadiers and chasseurs), and the 6 bns were dispersed for garrison duties. During the crisis of 1848 a new 4th Regt was formed, and a regimental depot was added to each.

Under the new 1852 structure, 2 regts each had a depot and 2 bns, each with 6 cos of fusiliers and 2 flank companies. An additional independent light infantry bn was formed, the *Cacciatori Indigeni* (National Chasseurs), with a depot and 8 companies. The reorganization was completed by 2 garrison bns structured like the chasseur unit; in 1859 one of these was disbanded, and replaced by a 2nd Bn

2   For Papal household corps, see commentary to Plate A4.

of *Cacciatori Indigeni*. A final reorganization, conducted by Gen Kanzler following the defeat at Castelfidardo, reduced the national infantry to one line regiment and one battalion of *cacciatori*, their internal structure remaining unchanged.

Foreign infantry
After the Liberal revolts of 1830–31, when many Papal soldiers had joined forces with the patriots against the Austrian intervention, the Papacy began recruiting in Switzerland. Unlike the Neapolitans, however, they did not conclude agreements with the various cantons, but asked two Swiss aristocrats each to raise a regiment. Despite being almost entirely Swiss, these were titled *Esteri* (Foreign); each had 2 bns each of 6 cos (4 of fusiliers and 1 each of grenadiers and voltigeurs). The two regts formed the *Brigata Estera*, which in 1833 received an 8-gun company/ battery of foreign artillery. The 1849 Roman Republic disbanded the Foreign Bde, but in 1852 both regiments were re-raised, now with depots and 2 bns of 8 companies.

In 1859, after the Swiss units of the Neapolitan Army were disbanded following a mutiny, many of their soldiers sought new employers. The Papal authorities used these veterans to form a new light battalion of *Carabinieri Esteri* with 8 companies. After Castelfidardo, the two Foreign Regts were finally disbanded, but the Foreign Carabineers continued to serve; in 1868 the unit was expanded into a regiment with 2 bns, each with a depot and 6 active companies.

Cavalry
In 1847 the one Regiment of Dragoons had 6 squadrons and the Mounted Chasseurs just 2 squadrons. For the campaign of 1848 against Austria the latter was expanded to 6 sqns and redesignated 2nd Regt of Dragoons. After the Republican period the cavalry was reduced to a single Dragoon Regt with a depot and 5 squadrons. With the loss in 1859 of the Papal Legations that it was garrisoning, most of the unit passed to the Piedmontese Army. Consequently, in 1860 the regiment was re-formed with 2 sqns, the second being composed of foreign volunteers. A 3rd Sqn was added in 1867, and a 4th in 1870.

Artillery and Engineers
Previously the Papal artillery was organized in 6 independent companies/ batteries (4 foot and 2 mounted), plus a company of artificers, while the Engineer Corps was a small all-officer unit. During the 1848 campaign the Engineers were expanded by the creation of two sapper companies. Under the 1852 reorganization a single artillery regiment had a depot and 8 cos (5 field and 3 mounted), while the Engineers were again reduced to a few officers only.

In 1860, mobilization for the war against Piedmont saw the artillery expanded to 11 cos/btys (5 foot and 6 mtd, 2 of the latter being foreign volunteers), plus a company of artillery workers. In 1866, after the final reorganization, the Artillery Corps included 7 cos/btys (3 foot, 2 mtd, plus 2 depot) and a 'train' company (artillery transport). The Engineer Corps comprised a few officers and one sapper company. Finally, a new battery of mountain guns was formed in 1868, its ordnance being funded by a large donation from French Catholics.

Volunteer units

During the campaign of 1848 the regular Papal forces were supported by a series of volunteer units, totalling 8 battalions and 2 independent companies: *Battaglione dell'Alto Reno, Battaglione del Basso Reno, Battaglione delle Romagne, Battaglione di Ravenna, Battaglione di Lugo, Battaglione di Pesaro, Battaglione di Gubbio, Battaglione di Faenza, Compagnia di Ferrara* (later *Bersaglieri del Po*) and *Compagnia di Faenza.*

In addition, an independent division entirely formed with National Guardsmen, known as the *Divisione Volontari*, comprised the following units: 1st Legion of Mobilized National Guard (also known as 'Roman Legion'); 2nd, 3rd & 4th Legions of Mob Nat Gd; 1st Regt of Volunteers (mostly students); 2nd & 3rd Regts of Volunteers; and the *Tiragliatori Romani.* Six of the eight had two battalions each, the 4th Legion of Mob Nat Gd and the *Tiragliatori Romani* having only one.

To meet the Piedmontese threat in 1860 several new light units were formed with foreign volunteers, as follows:

Battalion of St Patrick Created on 12 June 1860 from Irish volunteers, this 8-company unit fought with great distinction; after the defeat of Castelfidardo the survivors were grouped into a single company, which was finally disbanded in 1862.

Austrian Bersaglieri After Austria's defeat in the Second War of Unification it could not send the Papacy direct military aid, but the Austrian authorities sponsored the recruitment of volunteers in their territories. Five Austrian light infantry battalions were formed with from 4 to 8 cos each, and known as *Bersaglieri* in imitation of the elite Italian sharpshooter battalions. The backbone was provided by 80 officers from the Imperial Army who received special permission to serve for three years in the Papal Army. After Castelfidardo, in October 1860 the surviving Austrian volunteers were assembled into a single battalion, which was disbanded shortly afterwards.

Papal Zouaves Initially formed as a 'Company of Franco-Belgian Tirailleurs' on 23 May 1860, this was soon expanded to an 8-company battalion after incorporating a small volunteer corps known as the 'Crusaders of Cathelineau'. The entirely French and Belgian volunteers were mostly young aristocrats and gentlemen from the most traditionalist sections of Catholic society. After distinguishing themselves in 1860, the Tirailleurs were transformed into the famous Papal Zouaves on 1 January 1861. This highly motivated and hard-trained unit soon became the elite of the Papal Army, being in many ways a mirror-image of Garibaldi's Red Shirts. A continuous flow of foreign volunteers allowed enlargement into a 2-bn regiment in 1867. After the victory of Mentana the Zouaves became even more celebrated throughout Catholic Europe, and hundreds of new volunteers flocked to join the 'defenders of the Pope'. The Franco-Belgian component was gradually outnumbered by other nationalities (counter-intuitively, Dutch volunteers became the largest single group). In the last months of 1867 the Regt of Zouaves formed a 3rd Bn, and a 4th in 1868, each with one depot and 6 active companies.

Sub-lieutenant, Papal Zouaves, 1861; officers had a completely different uniform from that of their men (see Plate B1). Colours: black busby with red top; national cockade; white plume; gold badge of Papal crown-and-keys coat of arms, gold cords and tasseled flounders. Light blue jacket with black lace and embroidered tracery to front and cuffs; rear seam vent of forearms with lace and ball buttons, in style of French officers' undress *tenue d'Afrique;* gold Hungarian knots on sleeves. Light blue *veste* with black decoration; light blue 'Turkish' trousers with black piping and knots; gold sword belt over red sash; black sword knot and gold tassel; black boots with dark brown fold-over tops.

In 1870 the Zouaves were the only troops to attempt a serious defence of Rome against the Italians. When the unit was finally disbanded its 760 French survivors became the core of the new 2-bn *Légion de Volontaires de l'Ouest*, which fought with conspicuous courage against the Prussians.

Legion of Antibes This unit (aka the 'Roman Legion') was named for the city in southern France where it was formed. It was created on 8 September 1866 with the help of Napoleon III, as a replacement for the French occupation corps that left Rome that year. In order to attract recruits from the French regular forces, Napoleon ordered that volunteers would retain their French nationality and that their period of service in the Papal Army would count as if performed in the French Army. The Legion initially had 6 light infantry companies, later expanded to 8; after Mentana, it was expanded to 2 bns each with 1 depot and 6 active companies. On the outbreak of the Franco-Prussian War any volunteers wishing to defend their own country were released, and consequently the 5th and 6th Cos of each battalion were disbanded.

Police

Additionally, in 1847 the Pope could call on three paramilitary corps for maintaining internal security: the *Carabinieri* (gendarmerie), the *Bersaglieri Pontifici* (Papal Sharpshooters) and the *Guardia di Finanza* (Finance Guard). In general terms we might describe the *Carabinieri* as a militarized police force, the *Bersaglieri Pontifici* as a conventional police force, and the *Guardia di Finanza* as an armed customs service.

The *Carabinieri* were organized in a single regiment of 6 squadrons; the 1st Sqn was stationed in Rome, and had two additional companies, one 'chosen' and the other serving at the Apostolic Palace. The *Bersaglieri Pontifici* and *Guardia di Finanza* were dispersed throughout the Papal States. On 22 May 1848 the *Bersaglieri Pontifici* were absorbed into the *Carabinieri*, which expanded to two regiments. In 1850 the *Carabinieri* were transformed into a new *Gendarmeria* corps of 3 mounted sqns and 14 foot companies. In 1860 the Gendarmerie was reorganized as two static Territorial Legions and a mobile force composed of a foot battalion and two mounted squadrons. After the final reorganization of 1866 the Gendarmerie had 12 foot cos (10 static and 2 mobile), one mounted sqn and a depot.

Auxiliary corps

Finally, the Papal Army of 1870 included the *Truppe Volontarie di Riserva*, the *Volontari Pontifici della Riserva* and the *Squadriglieri*.

The 'Volunteer Troops of the Reserve' were formed during the military emergency of 1860, as a general militia. In case of emergency each province had to raise an infantry battalion, with from 4 to 8 companies. After 1861 they were mobilized only very rarely and on a limited scale. The 'Papal Volunteers of the Reserve' were formed on 11 February 1869, with volunteers from the minor nobility or wealthy bourgeoisie; there were initially 3 companies, to be augmented in case of mobilization to 6 or 8.

Unlike these Volontari, the Squadriglieri were an elite, recruited from experienced hunters and 'backwoodsmen'. These semi-regular auxiliaries were recruited for the specific purpose of suppressing brigands and insurgents in the hills of the southern Papal provinces, where this

Bugler, volunteer Legion of Antibes, 1866. Colours: dark blue shako with yellow top band, piping and lace loop to national cockade; green pompon, black falling plume. Dark blue tunic with yellow collar and piping to front and pointed cuffs; additional musician's braid on collar and cuffs; green epaulettes with yellow crescents. *Garance*-red trousers with dark blue stripes, white spat-gaiters and black shoes. Black leather French M1845 light infantry equipment.

scourge had spread from the former territories of the Kingdom of the Two Sicilies. The Squadriglieri were under the orders of the Gendarmerie and had no officers or NCOs of their own; they totalled some 250, organized in ten local detachments.

Weapons

In 1848 the Papal infantry were equipped with M1822 French muskets converted from flintlock to percussion, of which 24,000 were purchased from 1847. After 1849 they received new M1842 French percussion muskets, which were used until 1869. In that year the line infantry received Remington breech-loading 'rolling-block' M1867 rifles, manufactured in Belgium or England. Until the reorganization of 1850–52 light infantry were equipped with the same muskets as the line units, and in 1857 they received a locally produced copy of the contemporary French model, known as *carabina Mazzocchi* M1857 and mounting a 'yataghan' bayonet. After 1860 the light infantry was re-equipped with French M1853s, replaced in 1868 by the new Remington rifles. The Legion of Antibes and the Papal Zouaves had the same weapons and followed the same changes as the other light infantry units.

The Dragoons and Mounted Chasseurs of 1848 were armed with M1822 French sabres, respectively of the straight heavy cavalry and curved light cavalry models. Mounted Chasseurs also had French M1822 converted percussion carbines, while the Dragoons carried a pair of pistols. During 1860–70 the Dragoons received different models of carbines; it was only in 1870 that Remington 'rolling-blocks' were adopted as standard. Officers of all units armed themselves, usually with Lefaucheaux revolvers.

The Papal artillery of 1847 could deploy just one field battery with 8 old Gribeauval pieces; during 1848 two more field batteries were hastily equipped, one with 8 and one with 6 guns. After the disasters of 1848–49 the artillery had to be completely rebuilt. By 1860 all companies/batteries deployed 6 French guns of the following mixed types: La Hitte bronze and rifled 6-pdr field guns, M1859 4-pdr mountain guns, 18-pdr heavy guns and 12-pdr howitzers. The new mountain battery created in 1868 had 6 rifled 6-pdrs, transported on mules. The individual weapon of foot artillerymen was a shortened musket, while mounted gunners carried a sabre and a pistol. No standard patterns were issued before 1870, when all artillerymen received the M1867 Remington artillery musketoon.

THE TUSCAN ARMY, 1848–59

In 1848 the previously stable and prosperous Grand Duchy of Tuscany, governed by Leopold II of the House of Habsburg-Lorraine, saw shattering political changes. On 11 February, under strong public pressure, Leopold conceded a constitution, and on 21 March Tuscany joined Piedmont in the war against Austria. Its small army was augmented by large volunteer units, and at Curtatone and Montanara (29 May) it was the stubborn Tuscan force that saved the Piedmontese Army from complete destruction. However, following the Austrian victory at Custoza (27 July) and Piedmont's signing of the Armistice of Salasco (9 August), a 'Democratic' revolt against the grand duke broke out in Livorno, Tuscany's major port, on 25 August.

Leopold was obliged to accept a new Democratic government, but on 30 January 1849 he abandoned Florence and went into exile under Bourbon protection, alongside the Pope. On 15 February the Democrats proclaimed a Tuscan Republic, but after Piedmont's defeat at Novara (23 March) the city of Florence rose against the Republic with the support of the army and National Guard. A new regime invited Leopold II to resume the throne, but Livorno declared a breakaway Democratic government. Leopold requested Austrian military help, and on 11 May, after a siege and hard fighting, Tuscan and Austrian forces recaptured Livorno. On 28 July, Leopold II returned to Florence; the National Guard was disbanded and Austrian troops remained in Tuscany until spring 1855.

In 1859 the grand duke proclaimed his neutrality in the Second War between Piedmont and Austria, but both the populace and the army were strongly in favour of siding with Piedmont. On 27 April 1859 Leopold II was obliged to abandon Florence once again; a provisional government was formed, which offered the suzerainty of Tuscany to Victor Emmanuel II of Piedmont. On 29 May the provisional government allied itself with Piedmont and France. On 6 July a joint force of French V Corps with a Tuscan division reached the theatre of operations, but hostilities ended just two days later.

ORGANIZATION:

Regular army
Household troops comprised the *Real Guardia del Corpo*, a mounted guard of just 28 aristocrats, and the *Guardia Reale del Corpo*, a 62-strong foot bodyguard of elderly officer and NCO veterans stationed at the Pitti Palace. There were two line regiments, the 1st '*Real Ferdinando*' and 2nd '*Real Leopoldo*'; each had 4 bns (1 of grenadiers and 3 of fusiliers), but each battalion had just two companies. During 1848 a single light company was added to each regiment. The light infantry *Reggimento Veliti* had 3 battalions, also each with 2 companies; this regiment always had a dual character reflecting its internal-security background. The *Reali Cacciatori a Cavallo* (Mounted Chasseurs) had 4 squadrons. In 1849, shortly before the grand duke's temporary exile, a 3rd Line Inf Regt was formed.

The artillery corps had a total of 12 companies/batteries, divided into *scelte*, *del centro* and *di costa* categories. The 2 *compagnie scelte* were the only field units, totalling 300 men; the 6 *compagnie del centro*, totalling 720, were deployed in various defences along the Tuscan coast; and the 4 *compagnie di costa*, with 500 men, garrisoned the island of Elba off the coast. The 6 'centre' companies were the only ones grouped into a battalion, the *Battaglione Cannonieri Guardacosta Continentali*. A single train company was added only in 1847.

Additionally, the grand duchy had the Volunteer Chasseurs of the Coast and Frontier, a provincial militia performing auxiliary or police duties. These totalled 35 companies: 20 of *Cacciatori di Costa* and 15 of

Soldier of the National Guard, Grand Duchy of Tuscany, 1848. Colours: spiked black helmet with black falling plume, brass plate (arms of the grand duchy) and chinscales (from national cockade on left side); dark blue tunic with red collar, round cuffs, cuff flaps and frontal piping; brass epaulettes with yellow-and-red fringes; dark blue trousers with red piping.

Parade uniform of volunteer of the *Guardia Universitaria*, Grand Duchy of Tuscany, 1848. Colours: dark blue kepi with red bottom band and round badge bearing dark blue 'GU'; dark blue tunic with red collar, round cuffs and frontal piping; dark blue trousers.

Cacciatori di Frontiera. The companies of Coastal Chasseurs were assembled into 3 unequal battalions: 1st (1,200 men), 2nd & 3rd (900 each). The Frontier Chasseurs also formed battalions numbered 1–3, with respectively 600, 650 and 400 men. In addition, each of the 6 battalions had a squad of 18 or 24 light cavalrymen, these *Cavalleggeri di Costa* totalling just 160. There was also a small Finance Guard of customs police to control smuggling.

Under the short-lived Tuscan Republic a 4th Line Inf Regt was created and the *Battaglione Cannonieri Guardacosta Continentali* was augmented. After the Austrian intervention, the grand duke ordered a general reduction: the 4th Line Inf was disbanded, and the remaining 3 regts were reduced to 1 depot and 2 active bns each. (A new independent battalion of light infantry was created, but soon disbanded.) The artillery was reorganized into 2 bns, one of field and one of garrison companies; the first 2 field cos were classed as 'chosen', and stationed in Florence.

In the months following May 1849 Grand Duke Leopold carried out harsh repressions, with strong Austrian support; he even sent 4,000 of his soldiers to attack the Roman Republic (they took part in the siege of Ancona). A new *Imperiale e Reale Reggimento di Gendarmeria* was created, with the help of Neapolitan Gendarmerie instructors, specifically to suppress the activities of the patriots; this had 2 foot bns and a mounted squadron.

In December 1849, due to economic difficulties, the 3 line regts were replaced by a single regiment of 3 bns, each having 4 centre cos and 1 each of grenadiers and voltigeurs. The grenadiers of the disbanded regiments were absorbed into the *Reggimento Veliti*, which was reorganized with one grenadier and one carabineer battalion. The latter was dispersed in small detachments throughout the grand duchy to support the Gendarmerie, but in 1850 the carabineers were disbanded and the *Veliti* reverted to a single battalion. Some new small units were also created during this period: an Engineer Corps comprising a few officers only, and an independent garrison battalion stationed in the Tuscan Archipelago. Under a reorganization of 1852, the Line Inf Regt received a 4th Bn, while the 2 bns of artillery were assembled into a single regiment.

The last years of the grand duchy saw many changes. The line infantry was reorganized as 7 independent battalions, while the artillery formed a field 'division', 2 bns of garrison artillery, plus a body of artillery workers. In 1854 a new light infantry Bersaglieri Bn was formed, modelled on the Austrian Jägers; in 1855, 8th & 9th Line Inf Bns were added, and a 10th Bn in 1857. In 1855 a new company was added to the artillery field division, and in 1857 a certain number of sappers were put at the disposal of the Engineer officers.

National Guard and Volunteers
Leopold II had permitted the creation of the National Guard (*Guardia Civica*) on 12 September 1847, to channel the enthusiasm of restless civilian patriots. Since the most active of these were university students, on 10 November 1847 the grand duke ordered the creation of an

autonomous *Guardia Universitaria*, from professors (the officers) and students of the universities of Pisa and Siena.

When Tuscany declared war on Austria in 1848, it was decided to augment its small regular forces with active units raised from the *Guardia Civica* and *Guardia Universitaria*. Five National Guard battalions were sent to the front, from Florence (2), Livorno, Lucca, and one joint unit from Pisa and Siena. The *Guardia Universitaria* was transformed into a *Battaglione Universitario Toscano*, initially with 6 and later with 4 companies. In addition, the Tuscan expeditionary corps included an independent volunteer battalion from Livorno: the *Bersaglieri Livornesi*, or *Bersaglieri Malenchini* from the name of its commander. Despite their lack of proper equipment or training, these seven Tuscan units fought with great courage at Curtatone and Montanara. (It should be noted, however, that they were brigaded with the 10th Line Inf Regt of the Neapolitan Army – the only regular unit sent by the Bourbons to help the Piedmontese.)

Weapons

Until 1849–50 the Tuscan line carried French M1777 or British 'Brown Bess' flintlocks, gradually augmented with Brescia-built French M1822s. By 1850 all line units had received French M1842 percussion weapons, and by 1859 they had been re-equipped with the Pattern 1853 Enfield rifle as standard. In 1852 the light infantry received M1851 Federal Swiss rifles. The Mounted Chasseurs were armed with French M1822 light cavalry sabres and flintlock carbines until 1849; upon transformation into a regiment that year they received Piedmontese M1833/36 lances, M1843 musketoons and M1834 sabres. At Curtatone and Montanara in 1848 the artillery could only deploy 9 serviceable Gribeauval pieces. From the reorganization of 1850 until 1859 all field batteries had 6x 6-pdr guns and 2 howitzers.

Officer (left) and rankers of Mounted Chasseurs, Grand Duchy of Tuscany, 1859, uniformed according to the 1852 regulations. Colours: white metal helmet, black fur, brass comb and frontal plate, brass chinscales, national cockade on left side; dark blue tunic with red collar, round cuffs and piping to shoulder straps, front and bottom edges; grey trousers with red double side-stripes.

THE ARMY OF MODENA, 1848–59

The small Duchy of Modena, ruled by the House of Habsburg-Este, had always been closely overseen by Austrian troops in northern Italy. On 21 March 1848, with the population of the duchy on the verge of open rebellion, Duke Francis V was obliged to go into exile; the patriots soon formed a provisional government, and organized a National Guard. During the few months of revolutionary government the duchy joined Piedmont's war against Austria and was occupied by the Piedmontese. After the Armistice of Salasco on 6 August 1848 these were replaced by Austrian troops, who restored Francis V to his throne. In 1849 the duke sent his infantry regiment to Tuscany, in support of the Austrian forces that likewise restored its grand duke.

On 11 June 1859, after the Franco-Piedmontese victory at Magenta, Francis V abandoned his duchy again, this time forever. After the brief transitional period of the Central Italian League (August 1859–March 1860), the Duchy of Modena was finally annexed by Piedmont.

Organization

In 1848 the little army of Modena included two small household companies (the aristocratic *Guardia Nobile d'Onore* and the veteran *Trabanti Reali*); one battalion each of line and light infantry; and small corps of dragoons, artillery, engineer officers and pioneers.

The line infantry *Battaglione Estense* had 4 fusilier and 2 grenadier companies. The elite light infantry, closely modelled on the Austrian Jägers, were named *Reali Cacciatori del Frignano* after the mountainous Appenine department where they were recruited. They had 1 depot and 5 active companies, but in case of emergency could call up numbers of partly trained men for a rapid expansion. The dragoons had a double function, both as soldiers and gendarmes, with a single mounted squadron and 3 foot companies. The artillery comprised 2 field companies/ batteries with a half-company of train, and 1 garrison company. A few engineer officers supervised 2 pioneer companies. In addition to these regulars, the Duke of Modena could also call upon a volunteer provincial militia. This could deploy a 4-battalion regiment from the province of Modena, a 2-bn regt from the province of Reggio, a 2-bn regt from the mountain departments and an independent battalion (6 cos) from Massa and the Lunigiana region. Shortly before his temporary exile, the duke authorized the creation of a National Guard, and also ordered the enlargement of the *Battaglione Estense* into a regiment with 12 cos (2 of grenadiers, 2 bersaglieri and 8 fusiliers).

Soon after the departure of Francis V the provisional government briefly disbanded the regular units, but soon reinstated them under different designations. The line infantry became known as the Regiment of the Line, while the dragoons were reorganized into a squadron of Mounted Chasseurs and a battalion of Chasseurs-Gendarmes. The *Cacciatori del Frignano*, the most conservative-minded unit of the old army, was not reformed. The pioneers were renamed *zappatori* and expanded into a 4-co battalion, and the artillery train was enlarged to a company. The provincial militia units were disbanded to form the new *Guardia Civica*. The provisional government sent the Regt of the Line to the theatre of war, together with a mobile column formed from National Guardsmen. This *Coorte Mobile Modenese e Reggiana* numbered 1,200 badly armed volunteers organized in 12 *centurie*, with just three artillery pieces.

After his return, Francis V naturally reorganized the army. The line infantry regiment had 3 battalions (1st & 2nd Bns, 1 grenadier and 3 fusilier cos; 3rd Bn, re-raised *Cacciatori del Frignano*, 4 chasseur companies). The dragoons reverted to a mounted squadron and 3 foot companies; the artillery had 1 mounted and 2 foot cos, but lost its train company; and the engineers and pioneers resumed their 1848 structure. The National Guard was briefly reorganized into 4 'Legions', but was soon replaced by a resurrected provincial militia, now in 3 regiments. In 1851 a 4th Bn was added to the line regiment (organized like the 1st & 2nd Battalions). In the same year the dragoon squadron was disbanded, its men being dispersed among the foot companies, to which a 4th co was added in 1855.

When the duke was definitively exiled in 1859, the entire regular army marched with him across the border into Austrian territory. Renamed the *Brigata Estense* as part of the Imperial Army, it served with the Austrian X Corps. Many young men from Modena refused conscription into the Piedmontese Army, and crossed the border to join the Brigade. This was finally disbanded in September 1863, without seeing action.

Weapons

In 1848 Modena's line and light infantrymen were both entirely re-equipped with French M1842 percussion muskets. In 1849 the *Cacciatori* received Belgian-made rifled carbines of the French 'Vincennes' model; in 1856 these were converted to the Minié system. In October 1848 mounted dragoons replaced their flintlock carbines with Piedmontese M1843 cavalry musketoons, but foot dragoons were armed with musketoons converted from flintlock to percussion. Mounted dragoons had Austrian heavy cavalry sabres, foot dragoons French infantry *sabre-briquets*. For the campaign of 1848 Modena could deploy just 3 elderly Gribeauval guns; after the duke's restoration the artillery was reorganized with 6 bronze 6-pdrs, 4 bronze 7-pdr Austrian howitzers and 2 bronze 10-pdr howitzers. After its absorption into the Imperial Army the entire *Brigata Estense* was re-equipped with Austrian weapons.

Duchy of Modena, 1859: chasseur from 3rd Bn, *Reggimento Estense*. Black Tyrolean hat; on upturned left brim black plume falling from national cockade, white lace loop, brass buglehorn. Grey double-breasted tunic with green collar, round cuffs and shoulder rolls; green piping to shoulder straps, front and bottom edges. Grey trousers with green piping; black equipment.

The disbanding ceremony of Modena's exiled *Brigata Estense* in Austrian service, 24 September 1863. From left to right: dragoons, artillery, sappers, line infantry and chasseurs. For most uniforms see commentaries to Plates D1 & D2. The sappers wore a black shako with national cockade, white lace loop and green falling plume; a dark blue tunic with red collar, round cuffs, and piping to shoulder straps and edges; red-piped light blue-grey trousers, and black belt equipment.

THE ARMY OF PARMA, 1848–59

The Duchy of Parma was ruled as an Austrian puppet state by the ex-wife of Napoleon, Marie Louise of Habsburg-Lorraine, until her death in 1847. She was succeeded by a Bourbon duke, Charles II, who had to face the crisis of 1848 just a few months later. On 20 March the population rose in rebellion, forming a provisional government. This organized a National Guard, and sent an infantry battalion plus a National Guard unit to join the Piedmontese forces. On 19 April Charles II abandoned his duchy, which was then occupied by the Piedmontese Army.

The Austrians entered Parma on 5 August 1848; Charles II soon abdicated in favour of his son, Charles III, who was enthroned in August 1849. The new duke greatly expanded the regular army; however, the damaging economic consequences of this programme caused deep anger, leading to his assassination in 1854, and thereafter the army was reduced. In May 1859 the population rebelled again, driving Duke Robert I into exile on 9 June. After the brief transitional period of the Central Italian League, the Duchy of Parma was annexed by Piedmont.

Organization

In 1848 the army comprised two small household companies (the *Guardie d'Onore* and *Reali Alabardieri*); one line infantry regiment; a corps of dragoons doubling as a gendarmerie, dispersed throughout the duchy; an artillery company; and a few engineer officers. The infantry regiment had 2 battalions, with 6 fusilier and 2 flank companies. The line battalion sent by the provisional government against the Austrians was later incorporated into the Piedmontese 25th Infantry Regiment.

The new National Guard was organized as 2 infantry 'legions', each having 5 bns of which the first 3 were active and the other 2 reserve. A battalion had 5x 120-man companies, and the legion from the city of Parma had an additional cavalry squadron. The unit sent with the regular battalion to support Piedmont was a 'column' of volunteers; later in the war a second column of mobilized National Guardsmen was also organized. In addition, two smaller groups of volunteers were absorbed into the Piedmontese Army, respectively in the 8th and 10th Bersaglieri Battalions. During the brief Piedmontese occupation the dragoons were absorbed into the Piedmontese *Carabinieri*, and a small body of sappers was put under the orders of the engineer officers. During the Austrian occupation the National Guard was disbanded, while the remaining battalion of line infantry lost its grenadier and chasseur companies.

The expansion ordered by Charles III was completed in 1852: *Reali Guardie del Corpo* (ex-*Guardie d'Onore*, now 3 cos) and *Reali Alabardieri* company; line infantry brigade (5 bns); *Real Corpo di Gendarmeria* (ex-dragoons, 4 cos); one artillery field co/bty plus artillery workers co; and engineer officers plus sapper company.

The battalions of the *Brigata Fanteria* varied in composition. The elite 1st Bn or *Guardia Reale* had 2 companies each of grenadiers and light 'musketeers'. The 2nd and 3rd Bns and the reserve 4th Bn each had 6 fusilier companies, and the elite light 5th Bn had 4 chasseur companies. The Gendarmerie company garrisoned in Parma city included a mounted half-squadron. The duke also created a 24-man troop of Guides, attached to the general staff. He also planned to replace the National Guard with new *Volontari Reali di Riserva*, but these Royal Volunteers of the Reserve were never raised.

After the death of Charles III the 1st and 4th Bns were disbanded and the 5th was reduced to 2 light infantry companies; the artillery workers were reduced to a platoon; and the sapper company was disbanded. In 1859 the entire army followed Duke Robert I into exile in Austrian territory, and was disbanded on 12 June 1859.

Weapons

Until 1851 Parma's line infantry had old French and British muskets converted to percussion; in that year all fusiliers received the French M1842. The 'musketeers' of the 1st Bn initially had old Baker rifles converted to percussion, but in 1851 received French M1842 light infantry muskets. The 5th (Chasseur) Bn was equipped with the French 'Vincennes' carbine. The foot dragoons/gendarmes had Neapolitan-made French M1842 light infantry muskets and *sabre-briquets* of Prussian type; mounted gendarmes used Italian percussion cavalry carbines and local copies of the French An IX sabre for the Imperial Gendarmerie. In 1848–49 the artillery was negligible, but Charles III re-equipped it at great cost with captured Piedmontese pieces bought from the Austrians: 2x 16-pdr guns, 6x 8-pdr guns, and 2x 15cm howitzers. In addition, 2 mule-pack 4-pdr mountain guns and 2x 12cm mountain howitzers were purchased from the Kingdom of the Two Sicilies.

Duchy of Parma, 1848: fusilier and grenadier. The fusilier's black shako has a white top band, red pompon, national cockade, yellow lace loop, and brass chinscales with star terminals. The grenadier's large black bearskin shows a national cockade and brass grenade badge, and both men display an Austrian-style spray of oakleaves. Their dark blue coatees have red collars, round cuffs and piping all around the shoulder straps and on front and bottom edges. The trousers are dark blue with red piping, the equipment white; note brass grenade and picker fittings on the grenadier's pouch belt.

Provisional government of Parma, 1848: National Guard.

Infantryman: white metal helmet, bottom half covered with black fur, with brass furniture and falling black plume. Dark blue single-breasted tunic with red collar, round cuffs and piping to front and dark blue cuff flaps; red epaulettes with yellow crescents. Dark blue trousers with red stripe.

Cavalry NCO: same helmet. Dark green double-breasted tunic with red collar, round cuffs and frontal piping; red epaulettes with white crescents; white rank stripes on red backing. Grey trousers with red stripe. Dark green shabraque with red border and white 'GN'. Both figures have black belt equipment. (Courtesy Anne S.K. Brown Military Collection, Brown University Library, Providence RI)

REVOLUTIONARY ARMIES, 1848–49

THE KINGDOM OF SICILY

Sicily was the first region of Italy to rise in open rebellion, on 12 January 1848, when the population of its capital city, Palermo, revolted against the Bourbon monarchy of Naples. After harsh fighting, events elsewhere persuaded the Neapolitans to withdraw their troops from the island (apart from the fortress garrison in Messina). A provisional government was soon formed, and the birth of the new state was proclaimed on 25 March. The Sicilian patriots had no intention of creating a republic, however, and searched in vain for a king to head a new constitutional monarchy. From 3–18 September 1848, with Austria victorious on the mainland, Neapolitan troops used their still defiant fortress in Messina as the toehold for recapturing the city after a siege and savage fighting. The following April they resumed a campaign of reconquest and repression, which effectively ended when, on 14 May 1849, they entered Palermo.

Organization

On 20 January 1848 the patriots of Palermo created a quasi-military organization (known as *camiciotti*, from the blouses they wore). The city was divided into 8 military districts, each of which had to furnish a certain number of insurgent squads (*squadre*) depending on its population size. On 28 January the formation of a National Guard was declared.

On 6 February, the Sicilian authorities started to organize a regular army. The single division was structured in two brigades, each with 4 battalions of line infantry (each 800 strong), a squadron of cavalry, and a field artillery company (see MAA 512, Plate F3 & 4). Additionally, 2 garrison artillery batteries were created, and subsequently one of the 2 brigade field batteries was transformed into a mountain unit. The original *camiciotti* were transformed into a sort of second-line light infantry, reorganized into battalions from the major cities: Palermo formed 6 bns, Catania 4, Messina 2 and Syracuse 1. Despite being raised largely from the poorest citizens and ex-convicts, the *camiciotti* units often fought with great courage, especially during the siege of Messina.

Over time, some new units were added: a small Guard for the general staff, and a few engineer officers with a sapper company. The regulars also included a 100-man company of naval infantry, and a *Battaglione di Cacciatori Esteri* (Battalion of Foreign Chasseurs) – ex-soldiers from various armies including Bourbon deserters.

These regular forces were supported by the National Guard, and by militia units known as *Compagnie di Cacciatori*. The *Guardia Nazionale* organized several battalions in each of the three major cities, Palermo alone mustering 12 battalions. There is also mention of mounted detachments known as *Guide a Cavallo* (Mounted Guides), young aristocrats or bourgeois who performed police functions. The 'Companies of Chasseurs' were created in the countryside as the rural equivalent of the urban *camiciotti*; these squads of peasants mainly conducted guerrilla operations in support of the regulars.

Finally, the Kingdom of Sicily sent a battalion of volunteers to northern Italy for the campaign against the Austrians. A similar unit, the *Battaglione Belgioioso*, was sent by the patriots of Naples, and took part in the battle of Curtatone and Montanara together with the Bourbon army's 10th Line Infantry Regiment.

THE LOMBARD PROVISIONAL GOVERNMENT

The insurrection of the 'Five Days of Milan' (18–22 March 1848), in which the ex-Austrian Finance Guard played a leading role, led to the formation of a provisional government. A week later Austrian troops withdrew into the Verona-Legnano-Mantua-Peschiera 'Quadrilateral'. During May the Lombard population voted in favour of annexation to Piedmont, but military defeats soon led to the Austrian occupation of Milan (6 August 1848).

Lombard provisional government, 1848: officer and soldier of the *Bersaglieri Mantovani Carlo Alberto*. Black hat with tricolour cockade; falling feathers in green (officer) and black (soldier). Dark blue tunic with red collar, pointed cuffs and piping to soldier's shoulder rolls; red embroidered cross on the chest; officer has silver epaulettes. Dark blue trousers with red stripe (officer) and piping (soldier). Black belts; officer's sword knot gold. (Courtesy Anne S.K. Brown Military Collection, Brown University Library, Providence RI)

Organization

The Milan provisional government ordered the formation of a National Guard, with each city quarter providing an infantry battalion and an independent light company of chasseurs. During April, in order to support Piedmont, the Lombards created 3 line infantry regiments: 1st (3 bns), 2nd (1 bn) and 3rd (6 companies). A depot battalion and a 4-company training battalion were also formed. Despite a disappointing response to recruitment, it was decided to form a 'Lombard Division' within the Piedmontese Army. This comprised 4 infantry regts (numbered the 19th–22nd of the Piedmontese line); 2 bns of Bersaglieri (the Piedmontese 4th and 5th); a dragoon regt (6 sqns) and one of light cavalry (2 sqns); 4 artillery btys; a sapper bn; and a small detachment of Carabinieri. Disbanded after the fall of Milan, the *Divisione Lombarda* was reformed in September to take part in the disastrous campaign of 1849. On 28 March 1849, after the defeat of Novara, the division was definitively disbanded.

Volunteers for the defence of the Venetian San Marco Republic, 1848: *Crociato Vicentino* (left) and *Volontario Pavese* (right). The 'crusader' sports a black ostrich feather in his brown hat. His light blue blouse has red collar patches and pointed cuffs, and an applied red cross on the chest; his trousers are of white and light brown ticking. The volunteer from Pavia has a black hat and feather, and entirely dark green uniform. Both have black belt equipment. (Courtesy Anne S.K. Brown Military Collection, Brown University Library, Providence RI)

Lombard volunteer units

These irregulars were numerous, and mostly employed in the northern mountains of the Trentino region. Assembled by the provisional government into the *Corpi Franchi Lombardi*, the volunteers were grouped into four large columns to invade the southern Trentino. After the complete failure of this operation by the Free Corps, the volunteers were reorganized into an Observation Corps (*Corpo di Osservazione del Tirolo*) with purely defensive functions. Giuseppe Garibaldi, just returned from his adventures in South America, joined the Lombard volunteers and led them during the last weeks of the 1848 campaign (15–27 August). At the beginning of September most were disbanded along with the rest of the Lombard forces. The following volunteer units were active in Lombardy: *Bande dell'Arcioni* (semi-regulars, whose commander would form another corps with the same name for the Roman Republic); *Bersaglieri Lombardi* (see under 'Roman Republic'); *Legione Polacca* (see under 'Roman Republic'); *Legione Ungherese* (110 Hungarians); *Bersaglieri Mantovani Carlo Alberto* (bn of 4, later 2 cos); *Bersaglieri Valtellinesi* (bn of 4 cos); *Cacciatori di Brescia* (regt of 2 bns, each 6 cos); *Colonna Vicari-Simonetta* (incl. light carabineer co, and 6 'bands' of semi-regulars); *Crociati Piacentini* (500 strong); *Battaglione Disertori* (Italian deserters from Austrian 38th Line Inf Regt 'Haugwitz'); *Battaglione Disertori Doganieri* (deserters from Austrian Customs Guard); *Guardia Nazionale Bergamasca* (2 bns); *Guide del Tirolo* (bn of 4 cos); *Bersaglieri d'Africa* (co of Italian

veterans of French Foreign Legion); *Legione Bergamasca delle Alpi* (light inf regt); *Prima Legione Lombarda* (2,000 strong); *Seconda Legione Lombarda* (bn of 5 fusilier & 2 flank cos); *Legione Trentina* (2 cos); *Cacciatori della Morte* (aka *Battaglione Anfossi* after commander's name – 600 strong); *Legione degli Studi* (students); *Veliti Leoncini* (bn of students, named after founder); *Volontari Bergamaschi* (bn of 5 cos); *Battaglione Malossi* (300 strong, from Brescia); *Battaglione Volontari Comaschi* (6 cos); *Carabinieri Svizzeri* (co of Swiss marksmen from Como); *Volontari Cremonesi* (300 strong); *Corpo franco Genovese* (Genoese co); *Battaglione Volontari Pavesi* (400 strong); and *Volontari della Valsabbia* (500 strong).

THE SAN MARCO REPUBLIC

On 17 March 1848 the city of Venice rose against the Austrian authorities; they obtained the release of the patriot leader Daniele Manin, and the following day the Austrians conceded the formation of a National Guard. On 22 March, National Guardsmen attacked the arsenal with the help of (mostly Italian) mutinous Austrian sailors, and captured 50,000 muskets. That evening the Austrian garrison abandoned Venice, but 3,000 Italian soldiers of the Imperial Army changed sides, together with part of the Austrian fleet. A provisional government soon proclaimed the independent Republic of San Marco, which within weeks controlled most of the surrounding region of Venetia. On 4 July 1848, the Republic of San Marco proclaimed its annexation to Piedmont, which sent its fleet and 3 infantry battalions from the Acqui, Savoia and Savona Bdes to Venice. These had to be withdrawn after the Armistice of Salasco (9 August 1848). After a siege lasting from 4 May to 22 August 1849, Venice was recaptured by the Austrians in the final act of the First War.

Roman Republic, 1849: mounted artillery NCO. Black shako with gold bottom and red top bands; red pompon and falling plume above tricolour cockade, gold lace loop, brass badge of shell over crossed cannons; brass chinscales. Dark blue tunic with red piping to collar, front, and top and rear of round cuffs; red epaulettes; yellow rank chevrons on red backing; red cords with tasseled flounders. Dark blue overalls with red piping, deep black leather 'booting'. (Courtesy Anne S.K. Brown Military Collection, Brown University Library, Providence RI)

Organization

The Republic's army included 8 'legions' of line infantry; 2 cavalry squadrons; a regiment of artillery; corps of engineers, sappers and train; a battalion of naval infantry, and the corps of naval artillery; the Gendarmerie, and the National Guard. In addition it could call upon many independent units of volunteers. The line infantry comprised the following:

1st Line Inf Regt, 2 bns (each 4 fusilier cos, 2 flank cos), formed from mobilized National Guardsmen.

2nd Line Inf Regt, 3 bns (as 1st Regt), mobilized Nat Gds; 3rd Bn disbanded April 1849.

Legione Euganea, 6 cos; volunteers from Padua, Vicenza and Rovigo.

Legione Galateo, 2 bns (each 6 cos) plus extra co of NCOs; volunteers from Treviso.

Legione Cacciatori del Sile, 2 bns (each 5 cos); volunteers from Treviso.

Legione Italia Libera, 2 bns (each 4 cos); volunteers from Treviso, Dalmatia and Istria.

Legione Dalmato-Istriana, 2 bns (each 6 cos); volunteers from Dalmatia, Istria and Hungary.

Legione Friulana, 6 cos; volunteers from Udine and the rest of Friuli.

The cavalry squadron had 2 companies. The arrival of 40 Neapolitan volunteer cavalrymen allowed the brief formation of a 2nd Sqn, but it soon reverted to 2 mixed companies.

The artillery regiment had 2 bns (each 1 field & 5 positional companies/batteries) plus a depot. Originally it had just 4 cos, but was augmented with volunteer companies: 2 each of *Artiglieri Ausiliari Veneti*, *Artiglieri Chioggiotti* and *Artiglieri Padovani*, and 1 each of *Cannonieri del Brenta* and *Cannonieri Buranelli*. In addition to this regular regiment there were also two independent volunteer units: the *Artiglieri Italiani da Campo* (2-co battalion of ex-Neapolitan artillerymen), and the *Legione Bandiera e Moro* (2 companies). The officers of the Engineer Corps were divided into *Genio Terrestre* (Land Engineers) and *Genio Marittimo* (Naval Engineers); they had under their command the Sapper Bn of 2 cos, later increased to three. The Train Corps had just two companies.

Ever since 1814 the Austrian Imperial Navy had been almost entirely composed of Italian personnel, based in Venice; as a result, as soon as the rebellion broke out the Austrian Bn of Naval Infantry and Corps of Naval Artillery (each with 6 companies) passed to the new Republic. The Gendarmerie was mostly made up of ex-Imperial soldiers of Italian origins, coming from the grenadier companies of their Austrian regiments. These were organized in a 'legion' of 7 companies, 1 of carabinieri and 6 of gendarmes.

Volunteer units

The volunteer units active in Venice itself were the following:

Cacciatori Brenta-Bacchiglione (2 bns light infantry, each 6 cos); *Battaglione Euganeo* (from Padua); *Battaglione Friulano*; *Battaglione Paschetta*; *Battaglione Prato*; *Battaglione Tornielli*; *Bersaglieri Civici di Schio*; *Cacciatori delle Alpi* (2 bns, each 6 cos); *Cacciatori Svizzeri* (Swiss marksmen co);

Crociate Veneziane (2 'crusader' units from Venice); *Guardia Mobile Padovana* (4-co battalion, mobilized Nat Gds from Padua); *Guardia Mobile Lombarda* (bn mobilized Nat Gds from Lombardy); *Legione Antonini* (500 Italians from France, 8 cos); *Legione Ungherese* (60 Hungarian artillerymen); *Legione Veneto-Napoletana* (2 bns, each 5 cos, ex-Neapolitan Army, commanded by Guglielmo Pepe); *Veliti Italiani* (4 'centuries' of students from all over Italy); and *Veterani Nazionali* (3-co veteran battalion). On 30 January 1849 most of these units were assembled into four large *Brigate Volontarie*, totalling 12,643 men.

The volunteers from the rest of Venetia formed the following units: 3 small artillery cos (*Artiglieri Friulani*, *Artiglieri Trevigiani* and *Artiglieri Vicentini*); *Civica Vicentina* (Nat Gd of Vicenza: 4 inf cos, mtd detachment, platoon gendarmes); *Crociati Padovani* (1,700-strong 'legion', mostly students, from Padua); *Crociati Vicentini* (350 men: 2 cos each of fusiliers and *cacciatori*); *Legione Trevigiana* (2 bns from Treviso); *Milizie Cadorine* (5 cos semi-regulars); and *Bersaglieri Universitari* (student bn from universities of Padua and Pavia).

THE ROMAN REPUBLIC

On 9 May 1848 the Papal Army in northern Italy, led by Gen Giovanni Durando, was defeated by the Austrians. The Pope, who had joined the Piedmontese only under public pressure, ordered its retreat, but significant numbers of troops decided to stay and continue the fight. The populace of the Papal States were of the same mind; on 15 November the Pope's Prime Minister Rossi was assassinated and citizens assaulted the Pope's residence. On 24 November, Pius IX abandoned Rome and went to Gaeta under protection of the Bourbons. On 9 February 1849 the patriots proclaimed the Roman Republic, including all the territories of the Papal States. The new state was soon invaded by Austrian, French, Spanish and Neapolitan troops. To face the emergency the Republican government formed a Triumvirate including Giuseppe Mazzini. After driving back the first French assault, and making a victorious sortie that knocked the Neapolitans out of the campaign, a heroic month-long defence ended when Rome was finally occupied by French troops on 2 July 1849. Garibaldi, who had been the main military leader of the Republic, continued his fight across the territories of the ex-Papal States until the end of that month.

Organization

By 7 December 1848 the new Republic had reorganized the regular forces (see above, 'The Army of the Papal States') as follows: 4 line infantry regts, a Bersaglieri bn (ex-6th Fusilier Bn), 2 dragoon regts, and artillery and engineer corps.

Each line regiment had 1 depot and 2 active bns; depot bns had 4 fusilier cos, active bns 6 of fusiliers plus 2 flank companies. The 8-company Bersaglieri unit was known both as *Battaglione Pietramellara*, after its commander, and *Battaglione Bersaglieri del Reno*, from a river near Bologna; many of its soldiers were in fact ex-convicts from that city's prisons. The 2 dragoon regiments had 6 sqns each. The single

Roman Republic, 1848: National Guardsman. This was the first *Guardia Civica* formed in Italy, in 1847, and many subsequent patriotic formations – in the Kingdom of Sicily, San Marco Republic, Tuscany and Parma – copied its Prussian-style uniform. Colours: spiked black helmet with red falling plume and brass furniture; after the proclamation of the Republic the original plate with the Papal arms and cypher 'Pio IX' was sometimes replaced with one showing the Imperial eagle. Dark blue tunic with red collar, round cuffs, and red piping to front and dark blue cuff flaps; brass contre-epaulettes. Summer white, or winter dark blue trousers with red piping. Black belt with brass buckle plate bearing 'GC'.

23

artillery regiment comprised a depot company; 1 positional, 4 field, and 6 garrison cos/btys; a pontoon company, a train sqn, and a veterans company. The engineers had a 4-company bn of sappers-miners and a company of sappers-drivers. In addition to the above, the Republic could count on 2 regts of Carabineers and the Finance Guard.

In April 1849 the return of many ex-Papal soldiers from the northern front, mobilization of National Guardsmen and regularization of volunteers allowed the formation of additional units. Seven new line regiments each had 2 active bns of 8 companies. The 2nd Regt of Dragoons was redesignated as the Regt of Lancers, with an unchanged structure. The artillery regiment was reorganized in 10 batteries: 2 mounted, 6 foot and 2 mountain. The battalion of sappers-miners was expanded to 8 companies, the pontoon company was transformed into a battalion, and the train into 2 companies.

National Guard and volunteers

National Guard Authorized by Pius IX on 5 July 1847, in 1848 the *Guardia Civica* formed 4 mobilized 'legions' for the northern Italian campaign. One of these, the *Legione Romana*, was later absorbed into the regular army as the new 10th Line Inf Regiment.

In February 1849, the National Guard mobilized 12 new battalions. Rome and Bologna raised 2 each, and the other 8 provinces 1 each. The National Guard of Rome also included a mounted detachment of *Cacciatori Civici a cavallo* and an artillery battery. The Bologna National Guard also raised an artillery battery, and another was composed of ex-members of the Swiss artillery company of the otherwise disbanded Papal *Brigata Estera*.

Italian Legion This was the largest and best volunteer unit deployed by the Roman Republic, formed and led by Garibaldi on a nucleus of 62 volunteers who had served with his Italian Legion during the siege of Montevideo (Uruguay). The inclusion of many volunteers from the Papal Legations and recruited during the march across central Italy brought it up to 1,000 men. Once in Rome, Garibaldi was able to enlarge and organize the Italian Legion as 2 battalions (termed 'cohorts') of infantry and a cavalry squadron (known as the *Lancieri di Masina* after their commander). The *1o Coorte* had 5 companies (*centurie*), while the *2o* had six. When the Italian Legion reached its peak strength of 1,500, a 3rd Cohort was formed, and Masina's Lancers were reorganized in 2 companies.

Bersaglieri Lombardi Initially formed as 4 companies by Luciano Manara, these first served the provisional government of Milan and were later taken into the Piedmontese Army as the 6th Bersaglieri Battalion. After the defeat of Novara, Manara and his sharpshooters went to Rome to continue the fight. During its last months, the unit was expanded to a 2-bn regiment.

Garibaldi's Italian Legion, 1848–49 (from left to right): volunteer wearing first uniform (dark blue blouse and brown trousers) and armed with pike; volunteer wearing second uniform (red blouse and grey trousers) and armed with carbine; trooper of the *Lancieri di Masina*. See also commentaries to Plates F1 & F2.

(continued on page 33)

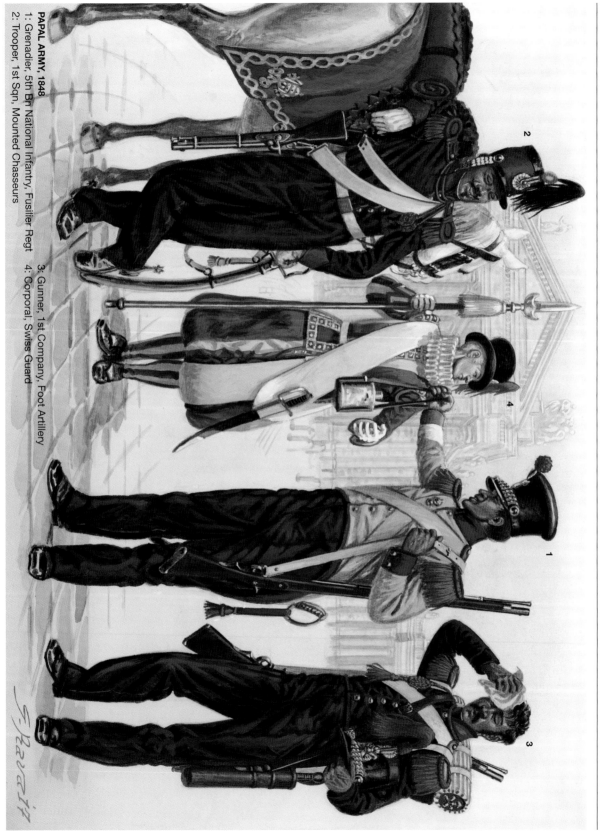

PAPAL ARMY, 1848
1: Grenadier, 5th Bn National Infantry, Fusilier Regt
2: Trooper, 1st Sqn, Mounted Chasseurs

3: Gunner, 1st Company, Foot Artillery
4: Corporal, Swiss Guard

A

PAPAL ARMY, 1860–70
1: Soldier, 1st Bn, Papal Zouaves, 1870
2: Soldier, Battalion of Saint Patrick, 1860
3: Trooper, Dragoon Regiment, 1860
4: Officer, Guides of Lamoricière, 1860

B

TUSCAN ARMY, 1848–59
1: Fusilier, 1st Line Inf Regt '*Real Toscano*', 1848
2: Volunteer, Tuscan University Bn, 1848
3: Soldier, *Battaglione Veliti*, 1859
4: Soldier, *Battaglione Bersaglieri*, 1859

C

ARMIES OF MODENA & PARMA, 1848–59
1: Fusilier, *Reggimento Estense*; Modena, 1859
2: Trooper, Corps of Dragoons; Modena, 1850
3: Soldier, *Battaglione Cacciatori*; Parma, 1854
4: Trooper, Guides of the General Staff; Parma, 1859

D

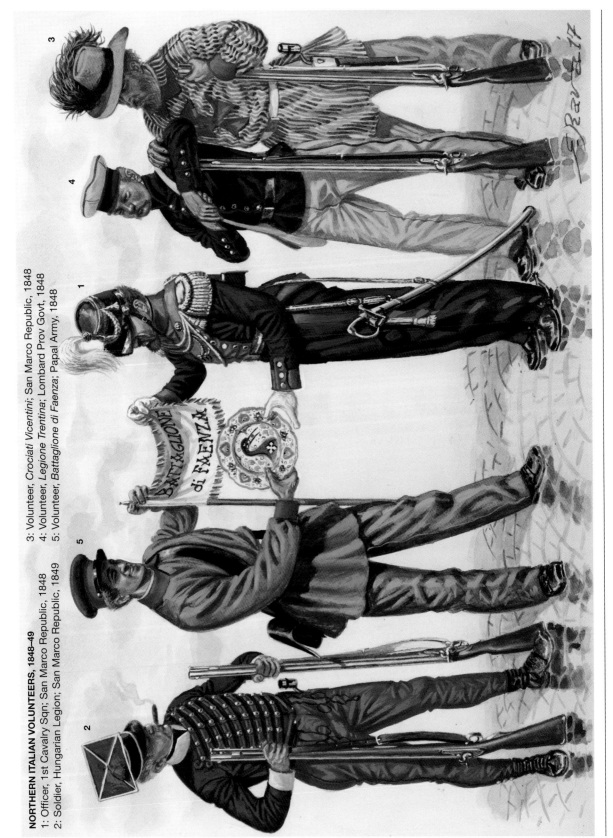

NORTHERN ITALIAN VOLUNTEERS, 1848–49
1: Officer, 1st Cavalry Sqn; San Marco Republic, 1848
2: Soldier, Hungarian Legion; San Marco Republic, 1849
3: Volunteer, *Crociati Vicentini*; San Marco Republic, 1848
4: Volunteer, *Legione Trentina*; Lombard Prov Govt, 1848
5: Volunteer, *Battaglione di Faenza*; Papal Army, 1848

E

F

ARMY OF ROMAN REPUBLIC, 1848–49
1: Volunteer, *Legione Italiana*, 1849
2: Trooper, *Lancieri di Masina*, 1849
3: Volunteer, *Battaglione Universitario Romano*, 1848
4: Volunteer, *Legione Polacca*, 1848

'RED SHIRT' INFANTRY, 1860–61
1: Officer, *Divisione Bixio*
2: Soldier, *Carabinieri Genovesi*
3: Soldier, *Brigata Medici*
4: Soldier, *Zuavi Calabresi*

'RED SHIRT' FOREIGN & MOUNTED UNITS, 1860–61
1: Soldier, *Brigata Dunne*
2: Soldier, *Compagnia Straniera*
3: Trooper, *Legione Ungherese*
4: Officer, *Guide a Cavallo*

H

Bersaglieri del Tebro Two companies of mobilized former members of the Finance Guard.

Bersaglieri del Po Initially a volunteer company from Ferrara that joined the Papal Army in northern Italy. Reorganized as a battalion with 6 cos, which took part in the defence of Ancona against the Austrians.

Battaglione Universitario Romano Formed by volunteers from the Papal universities of Rome and Bologna, on the model of the *Battaglione Universitario Toscano* (professors providing the officers and students the rank-and-file). Initially raised as part of the National Guard and named *Tiragliatori Romani*, with 3 companies from Rome and 2 from Bologna, it took part in the 1848 campaign in northern Italy. After the retreat of the Papal Army part of the battalion joined the patriots in Venice and the remainder went to Rome, where the unit was reorganized as the *Battaglione Universitario Romano* (of 5 companies). Meanwhile, in Bologna, another battalion of students was formed; later the two units were assembled into a *Legione Universitaria*, with 1st Bn from Rome and 2nd from Bologna.

Legione Polacca Formed of volunteers from Strasbourg and Polish residents in Italy, this was initially a battalion serving the Lombard provisional government of Milan. On 22 January 1849 the Polish Legion was absorbed into the Piedmontese Army, with the intention of sending it to Venice, but this plan was abandoned after the defeat at Novara. The Poles then marched south, briefly serving the Tuscan Republic before marching to Rome, where the remaining 2 companies took part in the defence of the city.

Legione Franco-Italiana Three small companies, aka the 'Foreign Legion', formed mostly of French volunteers who had already served briefly under the Tuscan Republic.

Squadre dei Sette Colli ('Squads of the Seven Hills') The poorest citizens of each of Rome's 14 neighbourhoods formed one of these semi-regular squads; they mostly performed security duties, but were also present at several combat actions. Initially all the squads were grouped in a single 'legion', later reduced to a single squad of 200 men.

Tiragliatori a Cavallo Three companies of Mounted Tirailleurs recruited among the famous cowboys of central Italy (known as *butteri*). These effective semi-regular light cavalrymen mainly served as scouts and convoy escorts.

Legione Toscana Single company of Tuscan volunteers, also known as *Legione dei Volteggiatori Italiani*, or *Legione Medici* after the name of its commander. Expanded to 2 companies, it played a courageous part in the defence of Rome.

Reggimento Unione Formed by assembling 4 volunteer battalions that pre-existed the proclamation of the Roman Republic: the *Battaglione Basso Reno*, *Battaglione delle Romagne*, *Battaglione di Ferrara* and *Battaglione Campano*. In April 1849 this unit was transformed into the 9th Line Inf Regt of the regular army.

Legione dell'Emigrazione Formed with volunteers from other Italian states now resident in Rome; 600 men in 8 companies.

Bande dell'Arcioni 300 semi-regular volunteers, in 9 'bands' named after their commander, recruited for rural guerrilla operations outside the city.

Brulottisti del Tevere A little corps of sailors/marines, who manned a river flotilla of small civilian vessels with improvised armament on the Tiber.

THE CENTRAL ITALIAN LEAGUE, 1859–60

As already described, during the tumultuous events of 1859 the armies of Tuscany, Modena and Parma followed different drummers. That of the Grand Duchy remained practically intact, and swore loyalty to the new provisional government formed under Piedmontese protection; those of the other duchies followed their monarchs into exile in Austrian territory, and were disbanded. Since it was not politically possible for Cavour to annex immediately the states of central Italy to Piedmont, they were temporarily assembled into a provisional confederation known as the Central Italian League. The main task of this puppet state, which existed only from August 1859 to March 1860, was to reorganize its military forces for imminent incorporation into the Piedmontese Army.

The Tuscan Army was reorganized under a new Piedmontese commander, Raffaele Cadorna; it then comprised 4 brigades of line infantry, 3 battalions of Bersaglieri, 2 regiments of cavalry, one of field and one of garrison artillery, and several National Guard units.

In Modena, Parma and the Papal Legations, numerous new volunteer units were created to replace the disbanded regulars; the most important of these was that known as the *Cacciatori della Magra*. Formed as a battalion during the spring of 1859, it launched a series of attacks on Modena's regular army shortly before the fall of Duke Francis V. Expanded with deserters from the forces of both Modena and Parma, it became a regiment of 2 battalions. A second regiment was then formed; the resultant brigade was then designated *Brigata Modena*, and finally absorbed into the Piedmontese Army.

All the volunteer units raised in Modena, Parma and in the Papal Legations were later assembled and regularized as a new 'Army of the Emilia'. This comprised 7 brigades of line infantry and 6 battalions of Bersaglieri; a squadron of Guides, one regiment of cavalry and one of Hussars; one regiment of artillery (with 9 field and 9 garrison companies/ batteries); a regiment of sappers; and several units of National Guard. In March 1860 both the Tuscan Army and the *Esercito dell'Emilia* (in total 52,000 men) were absorbed into the Piedmontese Army (see MAA 512 under 'The Piedmontese Army', by branch, from 1859).

GARIBALDI'S VOLUNTEERS, 1859–66

Cacciatori delle Alpi

During 1859, in the months before the outbreak of the Second War against Austria, thousands of volunteers from all over Italy arrived in Piedmont seeking to enlist in its army. The Piedmontese government, preferring to not include these men in the regular forces, decided to create an independent corps of volunteers, and Garibaldi was the obvious choice to be given command of these 'Chasseurs of the Alps'.

At the beginning of the war the volunteers comprised two regiments of light infantry (each with 2 bns of 4 cos); an independent battalion of *Bersaglieri Valtellinesi*, attached to the 1st Regt of Chasseurs; a squadron of mounted Guides; and a small detachment of elite sharpshooters, the famous *Carabinieri Genovesi.* (These were originally a shooting club founded in Genoa in 1852. They formed a 200-strong company armed with excellent M1851 Federal Swiss rifles for the campaign of 1859, but as the Piedmontese government suspected them of being extremist republicans only a small detachment of 46 joined the Chasseurs of the Alps. Garibaldi employed them as his personal guard, and they also followed him in his 1860 campaign.)

During the war this light brigade was expanded with new units: a 3rd Regt, an artillery battery, a company of sappers, and a section of train. Its initial success prompted the Piedmontese government to create a similar corps known as the *Cacciatori degli Appennini* as a large regiment with 4 bns, and in July 1859 this was absorbed into the *Cacciatori delle Alpi* as its 4th Regiment. In addition, during the same month the 1st–3rd Regts were also enlarged to 4 bns, and 2nd–4th Regts each received an attached independent company of Bersaglieri. A 5th Regt was also formed, but it completed training only after the end of hostilities. After the Armistice of Villafranca most of Garibaldi's men abandoned the Piedmontese Army; those who remained were reorganized into the new line infantry *Brigata Alpi* of 2 regiments.

'The Red Shirts'

The original 1,089 volunteers who disembarked in Sicily with Garibaldi in May 1860 were organized into 2 battalions, each with 4 companies of 120 men. In addition there were 23 Mounted Guides (initially without horses) and 43 *Carabinieri Genovesi.* A 9th Co was soon formed with young Sicilian volunteers, known as *picciotti.*

After the action at Calatafimi, Garibaldi's expedition began to receive official support from the Piedmontese authorities; they started to form in northern Italy large units of volunteers, which were gradually sent south to reinforce the Red Shirts. These reinforcements arrived in three

Sicilian *picciotto* (volunteer) from Palermo, 1860. These patriots who joined Garibaldi in Sicily were typically dressed in civilian clothes and armed with a motley variety of weapons, some of them improvised.

successive expeditions, known by the names of their commanders: Medici, Cosenz and Sacchi. The *Brigata Medici*, which arrived on 10 June 1860, numbered 2,500 men in 3 regiments, each of 2 bns of 4 companies. On 2 July, Enrico Cosenz disembarked with another 2,000 volunteers. It was with these forces, plus a large number of local volunteers, that Garibaldi won the action at Milazzo and completed the conquest of Sicily. On 18 July the Red Shirts were reinforced by the arrival of the larger *Brigata Sacchi,* which had 3 regts each of 2 battalions (see page 3).

Before crossing to the mainland to take the fight to the Neapolitans, Garibaldi expanded his original Mounted Guides into a 100-man squadron, and the *Carabinieri Genovesi* were gradually enlarged into an independent battalion of 300 marksmen. More importantly, he also reorganized what had now become an army to form divisions and brigades. Four divisions were named after their commanders: *Divisione Turr* (of 5 brigades), *Divisione Cosenz* (2 bdes), *Divisione Medici* (4 bdes) and *Divisione Bixio* (2 brigades). Each brigade generally comprised 2 or 3 infantry regiments, plus a certain number of smaller independent units; each regiment usually had 2 battalions, though with differing numbers of companies. The only brigade having a different organization was

Volunteer of the *Cacciatori del Tevere*. The 'Chasseurs of the Tiber' were a volunteer unit formed in Umbria for the campaign of 1860 against the Papal forces; they continued to serve until 1863, fighting against the brigands of the ex-Papal States. Colours: dark brown hat; white Savoy cross on tricolour national cockade, tricolour feathers. Light-blue-and-white ticking blouse; red collar patches, shoulder straps, round cuffs, frontal piping and pocket flaps on the chest. Grey trousers; white belt. (Courtesy Anne S.K. Brown Military Collection, Brown University Library, Providence RI)

the *Brigata Milano*, which formed part of Turr's Division; this was a sort of light brigade, with 3 infantry bns each of 4 cos, 2 cos of Bersaglieri, and an engineer section. The four divisions were numbered as if continuations of the Piedmontese Army's order of battle – Turr (15th), Cosenz (16th), Medici (17th) and Bixio (18th) – and each had an integral field artillery battery. After this general reorganization Garibaldi's forces started to be called *Esercito Meridionale* ('the Southern Army').

Once it was on the mainland, thousands of southern Italian volunteers joined Garibaldi. The 1,000 or so from Calabria formed an independent light infantry unit known as the *Zuavi Calabresi*, and some 2,000 from Basilicata were organized into the new *Brigata Basilicata*. For the Volturno River campaign in September–October 1860 Garibaldi commanded a

FAR LEFT
Infantryman of the Cosenz Brigade, which arrived to reinforce Garibaldi in Sicily on 2 July 1860. Colours: dark blue kepi with red bottom band and piping, brass buglehorn. Red neckerchief; light-blue-and-white ticking blouse with red piping to the fall collar and round cuffs. White trousers and gaiters; ticking haversack; black waistbelt equipment, and dark blue rolled greatcoat. (Courtesy Anne S.K. Brown Military Collection, Brown University Library, Providence RI)

LEFT
Bersagliere of Enrico Cosenz's formation, which grew to divisional size by the end of hostilities. Colours: red kepi with green bottom band and piping, brass buglehorn. Red cravat in throat of dark blue jacket with green standing collar, pointed cuffs, and green piping to front and shoulder rolls. Light blue-grey trousers with green piping, black boots. Dark blue rolled greatcoat. Black waistbelt with cartridge pouch; brass buglehorn buckle motif repeated on pouch. (Courtesy Anne S.K. Brown Military Collection, Brown University Library, Providence RI)

BOTTOM
Infantrymen and (at right) a *bersagliere* of the *Brigata Milano* in the *Divisione Turr* of Garibaldi's 'Southern Army'; this light brigade carried captured Austrian weapons during the summer-autumn 1860 campaign. The infantrymen have entirely white uniforms apart from a red kepi (left) and a black 'Calabrian' hat (and note that this man carries a slung shovel). The *bersagliere* has the same hat but with green feathers. His dark green blouse has a red front placket strip for the buttons, and red piping to the collar. Plain dark green trousers appear to be tucked into black laced anklets above his boots; the waistbelt equipment is black, and the rolled greatcoat grey. (Courtesy Anne S.K. Brown Military Collection, Brown University Library, Providence RI)

total of 25,000 Red Shirts, and in the months that followed more patriots flocked to his banner. They formed small additional units, usually termed *cacciatori*, which were of little military value.

Many foreign volunteers also travelled to join Garibaldi, and most of these were grouped into the *Brigata Eber* of the 15th Division. Commanded by a Hungarian exile, this included 5 battalions of line infantry, one of Bersaglieri, a Hungarian Legion, a Foreign Company, and a section of engineers. For the campaign of 1859 the Hungarian volunteers in Piedmont had formed a brigade with 4 infantry battalions; this had not been ready in time to fight against the Austrians, but some hundreds of these volunteers joined the Red Shirts in 1860. Garibaldi grouped them into his Hungarian Legion, which comprised a company of infantry and a squadron of hussars. The Foreign Company was formed with 100 Swiss deserters from the Neapolitan Army.

The only other distinct national contingent was British – an English Battalion and a British Legion. The first, initially raised as a 400-man battalion, was greatly expanded with Sicilian volunteers to the point that it became a 4-battalion brigade of 1,500 known as the *Brigata Dunne* from

Volunteer of the *Battaglione Bolognese*. This unit, also known as the *Cacciatori Bolognesi*, was formed for the 1860 campaign against the Papal Army; later it went to southern Italy to join the Red Shirts' fight against the Neapolitans. Colours: red kepi with green bottom band. Dark blue tunic with green collar and pointed cuffs; light blue-grey trousers with red piping; brown leather waistbelt equipment. (Courtesy Anne S.K. Brown Military Collection, Brown University Library, Providence RI)

RIGHT
Officer (left) and infantrymen of the *Brigata Eber* in Turr's Division (numbered 15th in the Piedmontese order of battle); this brigade was commanded by a Hungarian officer and mostly composed of foreign volunteers. All wear red kepis and red blouse-like tunics, the officer with light blue-grey trousers with red stripes, and the rankers with white. One has a grey greatcoat, the other a chasseur-style cape. (Courtesy Anne S.K. Brown Military Collection, Brown University Library, Providence RI)

the name of its commander. The British Legion, including both infantry and artillerymen, did not arrive in southern Italy until the campaign was virtually over, and remained unbrigaded.

On 11 November 1860, Garibaldi's Southern Army was disbanded. (For the inclusion of ex-Red Shirts in the new Italian Army, see MAA 512, page 17.)

Corpo Volontari Italiani

In view of the new conflict against Austria, on 6 May 1866 the Italian government decided to form a large corps of volunteers, to act independently from the regular army and thus requiring a balance of different kinds of units. Obviously, command of this Italian Volunteer Corps was given to Garibaldi. After completing its organization, the *Corpo Volontari Italiani* comprised 10 regiments of infantry (each 4 bns), 2 bns of Bersaglieri, 2 sqns of Mounted Guides, and a company of engineers. The line and light battalions had 4 companies each; the line were armed with old percussion muskets (French M1822T, M1840 and M1842), while the Bersaglieri had Pattern 1851 Enfield rifles. The 10 infantry regiments were later grouped into 5 brigades. In addition to the above, some regular units were attached to the corps: a 3-regt artillery brigade; a squadron of Carabinieri acting as military police; and a battalion of Mobilized National Guard for garrison duties. In total the Italian Volunteer Corps numbered roughly 43,000 men.

SELECT BIBLIOGRAPHY

Affinati, Riccardo, *Garibaldini Italiani 1838–1871* (Rome, 2009)

Affinati, Riccardo, *Soldati del Papa. Dall'antichità ai giorni nostri* (Rome, 2009)

Boeri, G., Crociani, P., Paoletti C., & Piana, P.G., *Uniformi delle Marine Militari Italiane nel Risorgimento* (Rome, 1997)

Brandani, P., Crociani, P., & Fiorentino, M., *La neuvième croisade 1860–1870* (Paris, 2000)

Brandani, P., Crociani, P., & Fiorentino M., *L'esercito pontificio da Castelfidardo a Porta Pia, 1860–1870* (Milan, 1976)

Brignoli, Marziano, *La Divisione Lombarda nella I Guerra di Indipendenza 1848/49* (Milan, 1988)

Carteny, Andrea, *La Legione Ungherese contro il Brigantaggio* (Rome, 2012)

Casali, Luigi, *Red Shirts: Garibaldi's campaign in southern Italy 1860* (Champaign, Illinois, 1989)

Cenni, Quinto, *Uniformi Italiane* (Novara, 1982)

Cesari, Cesare, *Corpi volontari Italiani dal 1848 al 1870* (Rome, 2013)

Di Colloredo Mels, Pierluigi Romeo, *Venezia 1848–1849: aspetti militari di un assedio del XIX secolo* (Milan, 2017)

Fiorentino, M., & Zannoni, M., *Le Reali Truppe Parmensi 1849–1859* (Parma, 1984)

Laria, Sante, *I fasti militari dei Finanzieri d'Italia* (Milan, 1930)

Menziani, Alberto, *L'Esercito del Ducato di Modena dal 1848 al 1859* (Rome, 2005)

Pieri, Piero, *Storia militare del Risorgimento* (Turin, 1962)

'Gli eserciti Italiani dagli stati preunitari all'unità nazionale', in *Rivista Militare* (Rome, 1984)

'Il soldato Italiano del Risorgimento', in *Rivista Militare* (Rome, 1987)

'La Repubblica Romana e il suo esercito', in *Rivista Militare* (Rome, 1987)

Scardigli, Marco, *Le grandi battaglie del Risorgimento* (Milan, 2011)

Scollo, L., & Compagni, P., *I Bersaglieri 1836–2007* (Bassano del Grappa, 2008)

Viotti, Andrea, *Garibaldi: The Revolutionary and his Men* (Poole, 1979)

Zannoni, Mario, *Le Truppe di Maria Luigia 1814–1847* (Parma, 2012)

Engineer (left) and soldiers of the train, *Corpo Volontari Italiani*, 1866. Colours (left): red kepi with green band and piping; brass badge of flaming grenade over crossed axes. Red shirt, piped green at fall collar, pointed cuffs and horizontally across chest; grey trousers piped red.

(Centre): same uniform apart from black hat, and dark blue waist sash under belt. (Right): civilian clothes, apart from red-piped grey trousers. (Courtesy Anne S.K. Brown Military Collection, Brown University Library, Providence RI)

PLATE COMMENTARIES

A: PAPAL ARMY, 1848

While the dress regulations of 1832 started to introduce a certain Austrian influence, this was combined with the traditional French styles which remained a distinctive feature of the Papal States' uniforms until 1870.

A1: Grenadier, 5th Battalion of National Infantry, Fusilier Regiment

The six battalions of national infantry were numbered in sequence but grouped into three regiments: the 1st and 2nd Bns formed the Grenadier Regt, 3rd and 4th Bns the Chasseur Regt, and the 5th and 6th Bns the Fusilier Regiment. The battalions had flank companies, and this man's white coatee and black shako are distinguished by the grenadier company's red epaulettes and pompon and the grenade badge on shako and crossbelt. His weapon is the French M1822 musket converted to percussion. The *Cacciatori* (chasseur companies) had yellow pompons and epaulettes and a buglehorn badge. Fusilier companies had no epaulettes or badge, and a medium blue pompon. The uniform of the Grenadier Regt was very similar to this, but with a large bearskin displaying a flaming grenade on the brass frontal plate and a red plume, and all companies wore red-and-yellow epaulettes. The Grenadier and Fusilier Regts had white coatees with medium blue collar, round cuffs and piping; the blue trousers were unpiped, and replaced by white in summer. The Chasseur Regt wore a dark blue coatee and trousers; collar, round cuffs, piping, epaulettes (worn by all companies) and trouser piping were all green. The shako, of the same model as illustrated here, had a green falling plume instead of the pompon, and lacked a frontal badge.

The two regiments of foreign infantry had the following distinctions: shako with pompon and standing plume in company colour (red, blue, or yellow) and no badge; dark blue coatee with yellow collar, round cuffs and piping; epaulettes in company colour worn by all companies; red trousers with yellow piping.

A2: Trooper, 1st Squadron of Mounted Chasseurs

The uniforms of the Papal cavalry and artillery remained quite French in style; this *Cacciatore a Cavallo* differs from his French equivalent in little other than the national cockade on the tall shako and the Papal coat of arms on the corner of the shabraque.

The Dragoons wore a black helmet with a brass comb and black fur roach, brass chinscales and flaming grenade frontal plate. Their dark green coatee had a red collar, epaulettes and red piping to the front and the round cuffs, and dark green trousers had red double side-stripes. The Carabineers' uniform resembled that of the French Gendarmerie: black bicorn with red pompon and white lace loop to national cockade; dark green coat with red collar patches and piping to the front and round cuffs, white epaulettes and aiguillettes; plain dark green trousers.

A3: Gunner, 1st Company of Foot Artillery

He too is practically identical to his French equivalent, but note the yellow epaulette straps.

A4: Corporal, Swiss Guard

This NCO of the *Guardia Svizzera* is distinguishable from the rankers only by carrying a spontoon instead of the traditional halberd. The yellow and blue colours of the uniform were chosen by the founder of the unit in 1506, Pope Julius II, and the red plume was added by Pope Clement VII (1523–34).

In 1848 the personal security of the Pope was guaranteed by the foot soldiers of the Swiss Guard and the mounted Noble Guard (*Guardia Nobile*). The latter, raised in 1801 by Pope Pius VII, was originally a heavy cavalry escort. Gradually evolving to perform a wider range of duties, it was formed from unpaid volunteers from the most important Roman aristocratic families. In 1848 the Noble Guard followed the Pope into exile at Gaeta; the Swiss Guard was disbanded by the 1849 Republican government, but was re-formed in 1850. On 14 December of that year Pius IX created a new unit for the protection of his person and of the Papal palaces. This *Guardia Palatina d'Onore* (Palatine Guard of Honour) had two 80-man companies, of volunteers drawn from the lesser nobility or upper bourgeoisie.

Artilleryman of the National Guard battery from Bologna serving in the Roman Republic, 1848. Dark blue kepi with red band and piping, national cockade, and brass crossed cannons (repeated on belt buckle). Dark blue tunic with red collar patches, and red piping to collar, round cuffs, frontal plastron and bottom edge. Dark blue trousers with red double side-stripes. (Courtesy Anne S.K. Brown Military Collection, Brown University Library, Providence RI)

B: PAPAL ARMY, 1860–70

In 1852 new dress regulations were heavily influenced by the contemporary fashions of Napoleon III's French Army. The national line infantry had a black shako with national cockade, brass frontal plate, black visor and chinstrap, top band and piping in company colour (red for grenadiers, green for fusiliers, yellow for voltigeurs), single company-colour pompon for centre companies or double for flank companies.

Artilleryman, Duchy of Parma, 1848. Black shako with gold top band, red pompon, national cockade, gold lace loop and brass shield with crossed cannons. Dark blue coatee with red collar and round cuffs, and red piping to shoulder straps and front and bottom edges. Dark blue trousers with red piping; white belt, gold sword knot.

The dark blue tunic had a red collar, round cuffs, cuff flaps and piping; the collar bore a dark blue company badge (star for fusiliers, flaming grenade for grenadiers, buglehorn for voltigeurs). Epaulettes were in company colour (red, green or yellow). Trousers were plain red. On campaign the tunic might be replaced with a shorter jacket having the same features, or with a double-breasted grey greatcoat in French style, with company-epaulettes and collar patches.

The *Cacciatori Indigeni* differed from the line infantry in having a buglehorn shako badge and green lace loop, green top band, piping and pompon. The collar, pointed cuffs and piping of the tunic were all green, the collar badge was a white buglehorn, while epaulettes were green with yellow crescents. Trousers were dark blue with green piping. The *Carabinieri Esteri* (Foreign Carabineers) were dressed as the *Cacciatori Indigeni* but with all their green distinctions replaced with yellow. The volunteer Legion of Antibes was also dressed like the *Carabinieri Esteri*, but with *garance* French-red trousers piped in dark blue. Apparently the *Bersaglieri Austriaci* were dressed like contemporary French *Chasseurs à Pied*.

The uniform of artillerymen included a black shako with red falling plume, pompon, lace loop to national cockade, top band and side chevrons, cords and flounders; brass crossed cannons, black leather visor and chinstrap. The short dark blue jacket had red epaulettes, collar patches, and piping to pointed cuffs, and dark blue trousers had red double side-stripes.

Among the Papal Army's auxiliary and reserve corps, the *Gendarmerie* had the same uniform as its French equivalent, with black bicorn hats (black bearskins for the mounted squadron); the *Squadriglieri* wore traditional civilian clothes (see Plate E4 in MAA 512); the *Truppe Volontarie di Riserva* were dressed more or less as the line infantry, while the *Volontari Pontifici della Riserva* resembled Austrian Jägers.

B1: Soldier, 1st Battalion of Papal Zouaves, 1870
The Papal Zouaves of 1860, still named the Company of Franco-Belgian Tirailleurs, were dressed as the *Carabinieri Esteri*, but in 1861 they received this grey uniform of French Zouave style. Note the buglehorn kepi badge; the gold brooch on the right breast reproducing the Papal coat of arms; and the red-laced rear seam of the forearms with many small ball buttons (see also figures B2 and B4). The weapon is a Remington 'rolling-block' M1867 rifle.

B2: Soldier, Battalion of Saint Patrick, 1860
French styles were generally apparent in the uniforms worn by other corps of volunteers formed for the campaign of 1860, and the silhouette of the French infantry regulations of that year is apparent here. However, the green-clad Irish volunteers had their own ornate variations including the shoulder rolls, royal-blue falling collar, and broad yellow inset lace down the front and round the bottom of the tunic. Note that this Irishman also wears the Papal brooch on his right breast, and is armed with the M1857 *carabina Mazzocchi*.

B3: Trooper, Dragoon Regiment, 1860
Again very similar to contemporary French style, except for the brass helmet plate of the Papal coat of arms.

B4: Officer, Guides of Lamoricière, 1860
This 40-strong cavalry company of young French aristocrats followed the new army commander Gen Lamoricière to Rome, serving with the General Staff and as an officer cadet

unit until disbanded on 9 November 1860. The *Guide di Lamoricière* had to pay for their own uniforms, weapons and horses, and adopted this elegant uniform echoing that of the contemporary French hussars, though with the Papal coat of arms badge on the kepi band.

C: TUSCAN ARMY, 1848–59

In 1824 the Tuscan artillery was the first branch of the army to adopt new uniforms of Austrian cut in place of the previous French Napoleonic styles, followed two years later by the cavalry. Finally, in 1835, the line infantry adopted the white uniform with which it took part in the First War of Unification (see C1). The National Guard and volunteers of 1848 wore completely different uniforms: the *Guardia Civica* received an elegant parade dress of Prussian style, copied from the uniform of the Papal National Guard; the volunteers were issued simpler blouses for use in the field.

The uniform of the Mounted Chasseurs included a black helmet with a brass comb topped with a red-over-white fur roach, brass chinscales, and frontal plate bearing the cypher of the grand duke. The dark green single-breasted coat had a red collar, round cuffs and piping, and the light blue-grey trousers had red double side-stripes. The uniform of the artillery was basically similar to that of the infantry, except that the coat was dark blue, the collar was black piped in red, and the shako plate showed crossed cannons.

In May 1848, the Tuscan Republic issued new dress regulations to the regular army, introducing local copies of contemporary Piedmontese uniforms. These were abandoned soon after the restoration of Leopold II, whose 1852 regulations were modelled on Austrian uniforms. In 1859, the fall of the grand duke brought no change apart from the adoption of the Italian national cockade, and the old Tuscan uniforms were also retained during the transitional period of the Central Italian League. The other troops of the League (those from the *Esercito dell'Emilia*) adopted completely new uniforms (see MAA 512, Plate C).

C1: Fusilier, 1st Line Infantry Regiment 'Real Toscano', 1848

The 1st Line Inf Regt had the collar, round cuffs, piping to the front and to the shoulder straps in red, and the 2nd Regt in light blue. The shako has a pompon in company colours (entirely red for grenadiers, and green for chasseurs), and a frontal plate bearing the ducal cypher 'LII'. The musket is a French M1822.

C2: Volunteer, Tuscan University Battalion, 1848

The Tuscan volunteers marched to northern Italy dressed in simple uniforms of this kind, including a loose, comfortable labourers' blouse in 'ticking' material with a falling collar in red or black. The majority of the volunteer units formed in Italy during 1848–49 wore blouses in light blue and white vertical striping; often, as here, they bore on the breast an embroidered or applied cross (the most common symbol of Italian patriots). The outfit was completed by a shako covered with protective oilskin, displaying a red pompon or a national cockade.

C3: Soldier, *Battaglione Veliti*, 1859

This elite unit of light infantrymen/gendarmes was always one of the best dressed in the Tuscan Army; note the double-breasted tunic with red collar (white braids hidden here), round cuffs, piping and shoulder rolls, and red trousers piped dark blue.

Volunteer for provisional government of Parma, 1848. Black *Bersaglieri* hat with national tricolour cockade and black feathers. Dark blue blouse with red collar patches, round cuffs, and front placket strip. White rank stripe on red backing; tricolour cross on the chest. White waistbelt equipment, and grey trousers. (Courtesy Anne S.K. Brown Military Collection, Brown University Library, Providence RI)

Officer (left) and junior NCO of the *Brigata Medici*, 1860. For colours of the soldier's uniform, see Plate G3; the forearm stripe is white on red backing. The officer has the same brown kepi and tunic with red piping and frontal placket strip. He has silver triple rank lace on his kepi behind a silver buglehorn badge, and as flat rings above the round cuffs. His trousers and gaiters are white, his greatcoat of a grey Piedmontese pattern. (Courtesy Anne S.K. Brown Military Collection, Brown University Library, Providence RI)

The line infantry uniform prescribed in 1852 was very similar to this, with some differences: instead of the falling plume the shako had a pompon, and a top band, in company colour (white for centre companies, red or green for flank companies), and a national cockade with a white loop instead of this brass grenade. The tunic was the same, but with no white braid on the collar and no shoulder rolls; trousers were light blue-grey with red piping.

C4: Soldier, *Battaglione Bersaglieri*, 1859
This unit, formed in 1854, was dressed exactly as the contemporary Austrian Jägers, in grey with green standing collar, round cuffs, shoulder rolls, and piping; note too the buglehorn badge below the cockade and loop on the turned-up hat brim, and the black accoutrements. The weapon is the excellent 10.5mm M1851 Federal Swiss *Feldstutzer* rifle.

Curiously enough, the Mounted Chasseurs were the only unit to retain the Piedmontese uniform adopted in 1848 until 1859; the artillery, instead, adopted a new dress of Austrian cut. This looked very similar to figure C3, except that the falling plume was black, and the brass badge was a flaming shell over crossed cannons; the tunic lacked shoulder rolls, and had a black collar and cuffs piped with red, and a gold

flaming-shell collar badge; and the trousers were grey with red piping.

D: ARMIES OF MODENA & PARMA, 1848–59
While the army of Modena continued to follow Austrian patterns during this whole period, that of Parma completely changed the style of its uniforms upon the succession of Duke Charles III: as his father had already done in the annexed Duchy of Lucca, he ordered the adoption of new Prussian patterns by the dress regulations of 1850.

D1: Fusilier, *Reggimento Estense*; Modena, 1859
Adopted under the dress regulations of June 1849, this line infantry uniform was very similar to that worn by contemporary Austrian infantry except for the dark blue colour of the tunic. Note, even, the typical Imperial practice of wearing oakleaves on the pompon. His weapon is a French M1842 percussion musket. The *Reggimento Estense* of 1859 comprised three fusilier battalions and one of chasseurs; the latter wore a uniform similar to that of Plate C4 except for minor details.

The artillery uniform was cut quite similarly to that of the infantry chasseurs, and worn with the same black Tyrolean hat, but displaying a black plume falling from the national cockade. The double-breasted tunic was dark blue, with black collar and round cuffs, and red piping to collar, cuffs and front. Trousers were dark blue with red side-stripes.

D2: Trooper, Corps of Dragoons; Modena, 1850
In this year the Dragoons were organized into one mounted squadron and three foot companies, but except for their equipment there was no difference in the uniforms of these mounted and foot gendarmes. The ducal cypher 'F.V.' was displayed on the helmet plate and the shabraque.

D3: Soldier, *Battaglione Cacciatori*; Parma, 1854
Under Duke Charles III, the infantry brigade of Parma comprised five battalions: one of Royal Guards, three of fusiliers, and this chasseur unit identified by its dark green tunic with red distinctions, buglehorn badge on the shoulder straps, and its knobbed helmet. The Prussian uniform style was absolutely dominant. Fusiliers differed in having a spiked helmet; all frontal plates displayed the duke's coat of arms, and chinscales attached on the left to the national cockade. Fusiliers had a dark blue single-breasted tunic with red collar, round cuffs and piping; solid white cuff flaps and shoulder straps, the latter with a battalion number embroidered in red; and the same trousers as the chasseur battalion. The tunic of the Royal Guard Bn was like that of the fusiliers, but with red shoulder straps and cuff flaps, the collar and cuff flaps having additional gold braid. Its two companies of grenadiers had a gold flaming grenade on the shoulder straps and the right crossbelt, and its two companies of 'musketeers' a gold buglehorn. The weapon is a French 'Vincennes' carbine.

D4: Trooper, Guides of the General Staff; Parma, 1859
In addition to the sabre the few Guides could also be armed with a lance, having a pennon in Parma's national colours (yellow over light blue).

While this uniform shows a certain Piedmontese influence (especially in the shako), that of the *Gendarmes* was perfectly Prussian. The white metal spiked helmet had a gilt frontal plate showing Charles III's coat of arms, and chinscales from the national cockade on the left side. The dark blue single-breasted tunic had a yellow collar, round cuffs and frontal piping, and white shoulder cords and aiguillettes; the light blue-grey trousers were piped yellow.

The artillery were dressed more or less like the infantry, in a spiked helmet with brass coat-of-arms plate and chinscales; dark blue tunic with red piping on the front and the top of the round black cuffs; red collar patches with brass badge of flaming shell over crossed cannons; brass contre-epaulettes; and light blue-grey trousers with red piping.

E: NORTHERN ITALIAN VOLUNTEER UNITS, 1848–49

The uniforms worn by the regular units of the Lombard provisional government were cut like those of the Piedmontese Army, but their main colour was dark green. The Lombard Division was dressed as the rest of the Piedmontese Army, but the tunics of the cavalry were dark green instead of dark blue; the dragoons had Piedmontese helmets while the light cavalrymen had dark green *bonnets de police* with red tassel and piping. Curiously, the artillery and sappers wore the same hat as the Piedmontese Bersaglieri. The three infantry regiments, formed before the organization of the Lombard Division, wore a dark blue kepi with red bottom band and piping, a light brown single-breasted jacket with red collar patches and piping to the front and the round cuffs, and light blue-grey trousers piped red. For uniforms of the Milanese National Guard, see MAA 512, Plate A4. The Finance Guard wore a black shako with national cockade, white lace loop and red pompon; a dark green double-breasted coat with light green collar, round cuffs, shoulder rolls and piping; and grey trousers with light green piping.

E1: Officer, 1st Squadron of Cavalry; Republic of San Marco, 1848

This elegant uniform in Piedmontese style differs in being dark green, as were those of all regular forces of the Venetian revolutionary republic, and displays the Lion of Saint Mark on the front of the shako.

The line infantry uniform was as follows: black shako with brass unit number, national cockade, and black falling plume from a red pompon; dark green single-breasted tunic with red collar, round cuffs, piping and shoulder straps; dark green trousers with red piping. The artillery uniform was similar, but with a *czapska* like that of figure E2, piped in red and with a brass crossed-cannons frontal badge, and trousers in light blue-grey with red piping. Sappers were dressed exactly like the infantry except for a black collar and a crossed-axes shako badge. The naval infantry and naval artillery both used the same uniform: dark blue single-breasted tunic with red collar, round cuffs and frontal piping, and dark blue trousers with red piping. Their headgear was a peaked cap: dark blue with red bottom band for the naval infantry, and reversed colours for the artillery.

The *Gendarmerie* wore a black bicorn with white lace loop, national cockade and a tricolour pompon; a dark green double-breasted coat with red collar, round cuffs, frontal plastron and piping; white shoulder cords and aiguillettes; and red-piped dark green trousers. The National Guard used uniforms in Prussian style, copied from those of the Papal *Guardia Civica*: spiked black helmet with brass Lion of Saint Mark plate and chinscales; dark blue single-breasted tunic with red collar, round cuffs and piping to front and dark blue cuff flaps, and red trousers with dark blue piping.

E2: Soldier, Hungarian Legion; Republic of San Marco, 1849

The volunteer corps fighting in the defence of Venice used a huge variety of uniforms, sometimes similar to those of the

Two small units of the Southern Army in 1860: the *Figli della Libertà* (left) and *Cacciatori dell'Etna* (right). The first was a corps of young orphans, while the second was formed by Sicilian volunteers. The boy is dressed in white apart from a red fez with a dark blue tassel. The older Chasseur of Mount Etna has a red kepi, dark brown jacket and light grey trousers. (Courtesy Anne S.K. Brown Military Collection, Brown University Library, Providence RI)

line infantry and sometimes quite improvised. The few artillerymen who served in the Hungarian Legion wore this elegant uniform in national style.

E3: Volunteer, *Crociati Vicentini*; Republic of San Marco, 1848

This simple uniform is representative of the dress usually worn by 'crusader' volunteer units: a ticking blouse with a fall collar, here with red collar patches, round cuffs and an embroidered or applied cross.

E4: Volunteer, *Legione Trentina*; Lombard Provisional Government, 1848

Most of the volunteer units formed by the Lombard provisional government used the traditional civilian clothing worn by the mountaineers of the Alps. This unit was an exception to the rule, being outfitted in a uniform of Prussian cut with a peakless cap.

E5: Volunteer, *Battaglione di Faenza*; Papal Army, 1848

This was one of the volunteer units formed in the Papal territories with mobilized National Guardsmen. Our volunteer is donating one of Faenza's famous ceramic dishes, with the city's peacock symbol.

F: ARMY OF THE ROMAN REPUBLIC, 1848–49

Like those of Milan and Venice, the uniforms of the regular forces of the Roman Republic and the secessionist Kingdom of Sicily followed Piedmontese models.

The Roman Republican National Guard's *Legione Romana*, later absorbed into the 10th Line Inf Regt, used a shako with a black oilskin cover bearing the unit's initials and a pompon in national colours; a dark blue single-breasted tunic (light brown in summer) with red collar and round cuffs; and light blue-grey trousers with red piping. The *Battaglione Pietramellara* was dressed like contemporary Piedmontese Bersaglieri but with light blue facings. The *Bersaglieri del Tebro*, by contrast, wore a brown Calabrian hat with a single black feather; a light blue-grey single-breasted tunic with red collar and cuff flaps, and red piping to the front, shoulder straps and round cuffs; and light blue-grey trousers with red piping. The Dragoons of the Roman Republic wore a steel helmet with brass comb, chinscales and frontal plate showing an Imperial eagle; a dark green single-breasted jacket with yellow collar patches, round cuffs and frontal piping; and light blue-grey trousers with yellow piping.

For uniforms of secessionist Sicily, see MAA 512, Plates F3 and F4. The *Cacciatori Esteri* wore a light green kepi with dark green bottom band and piping; a light green single-breasted tunic with dark green collar, pointed cuffs and frontal piping; and light green trousers with dark green piping. The National Guard had a spiked helmet with brass plate showing the island's *trinacria* symbol, chinscales and a red falling plume; a dark blue single-breasted tunic with red collar, round cuffs, and piping to the front and the dark blue cuff flaps; brass contre-epaulettes; and dark blue trousers with red piping. The *Guide a Cavallo* of the National Guard wore a dark blue kepi with green bottom band and white metal *trinacria*; a light blue-grey single-breasted jacket with green collar patches and light blue-grey trousers with green piping. The Sicilian volunteers sent to northern Italy had a white peakless cap with red bottom band and pompon, a brown single-breasted tunic with red falling collar and round cuffs, and red-piped brown trousers. The Neapolitan *Battaglione Belgioioso* wore a dark blue peaked cap with red bottom band, dark blue single-breasted greatcoat with red falling collar and round cuffs, and dark blue trousers piped in red.

F1: Volunteer, *Legione Italiana*, 1849

This is the second uniform used by Garibaldi's men, adopted from June 1849. The first had been similar to this, but with a dark blue blouse and brown trousers – all the other details, including the 'Calabrian' hat, were the same. Apparently Garibaldi initially lacked enough muskets to equip all his men, some of whom were armed only with pikes.

F2: Trooper, *Lancieri di Masina*, 1849

This exotic uniform of the Italian Legion's cavalry was clearly influenced by the dress of the French *Chasseurs d'Afrique* in Algeria, and the shako was frequently replaced with a red *chechia* (soft fez) with a light blue tassel; during cold months, the outfit was completed with a white poncho or large mantle. The *Tiragliatori a Cavallo* wore the traditional working dress of the *butteri* cowboys, their only distinctive element being a Calabrian hat with black feathers, national cockade and red band.

F3: Volunteer, *Battaglione Universitario Romano*, 1848

This elite unit was dressed in a smart dark blue uniform with dark green collar (with buglehorn badges), pointed buttoned cuffs, and trouser piping; the Calabrian hat had a dark green band.

The *Battaglione Basso Reno* had dark blue kepis with national cockade, red bottom band and piping; dark blue single-breasted tunics with red collar, round cuffs and piping

to the front and the dark blue cuff flaps; brass contre-epaulettes; and dark blue trousers with red piping. The *Battaglione Alto Reno* were dressed very similarly, but with double-breasted tunics and green facings. The *Bersaglieri del Po* were uniformed in a simpler way: black slouch hat with national cockade and black feathers; light blue blouse with red standing collar and round cuffs, and red cross on the chest; and dark blue trousers with red piping.

F4: Volunteer, *Legione Polacca*, 1848

This uniform, complete with a Polish *czapska* in red with a grey fleece band, was the most exotic in the Roman Republic's forces.

The *Legione Franco-Italiana* was dressed exactly like F3, but with red facings instead of green. The *Legione Toscana* had a dark blue peaked cap; a dark blue single-breasted jacket with a red-piped falling collar, pocket flaps on the chest and shoulder rolls; and red-piped dark blue trousers.

G: 'RED SHIRT' INFANTRY, 1860–61

Garibaldi's *Camicie Rosse*, being an entirely volunteer force, wore no regular uniform, and the first 1,089 volunteers who landed in Sicily were mostly dressed in civilian clothes. Gradually, however, some basic elements were adopted by all Red Shirts: a red kepi with green bottom band and piping, a red blouse or jacket with green facings, and blue or light blue-grey trousers with red piping. After the fall of Naples a large distribution of red cloth gave a higher degree of uniformity. The universal device of the *Camicie Rosse* was a buglehorn, since the entire 'Army of the South' was made up of light infantry units. Some large elements (like the reinforcement brigades led by Medici, Cosenz and Sacchi) wore their own distinctive uniforms coming from Piedmontese Army stores. For details of these, and the particular dress of some smaller units, see the captions to some of the monochrome illustrations.

G1: Officer, *Divisione Bixio*

This figure gives us a good idea of the uniform worn by many of the Red Shirts: red kepi with green bottom band and brass buglehorn (and here with officer's gold rank lace); red blouse with green collar, round cuffs, pocket flaps, and front placket strip; and blue or grey trousers with red piping, or plain white in summer. White summer kepi-covers, and various neckerchiefs, were extremely popular. Our young officer is armed with a Piedmontese sabre and a Lefaucheux revolver.

G2: Soldier, *Carabinieri Genovesi*

Garibaldi's crack marksmen were the only volunteers to retain in southern Italy the grey uniforms used for the campaign of 1859; note the black kepi band and piping, collar, pointed cuffs, hussar-style chest cords, and trouser stripes. The weapon is an M1851 Federal Swiss rifle. During the first phase of the campaign most of the Red Shirts were armed with old percussion smoothbores; when Piedmont started to support Garibaldi, the reinforcement brigades brought with them thousands of Enfield and Minié rifles, although the *Brigata Milano* was supplied with captured Austrian weapons instead.

G3: Soldier, *Brigata Medici*

This is a perfect example of the uniforms supplied to the reinforcement brigades: both the Enfield rifle and the rolled greatcoat come from the stores of the Piedmontese Army.

G4: Soldier, *Zuavi Calabresi*

The Calabrian volunteers adopted this combination of the red shirt – its green facings and white trim reflecting the national colours – with a Zouave-style fez and dark blue waist sash. The weapon is a Minié light infantry rifle-musket.

H: 'RED SHIRT' FOREIGN & MOUNTED UNITS, 1860–61

The foreign and mounted volunteers of the Southern Army were generally dressed in uniforms particular to their units; by contrast, the few artillerymen were indistinguishable from the infantry. At the beginning of the campaign Garibaldi's artillery comprised just five smoothbore cannon; it was later augmented with captured Neapolitan pieces, and by the arrival of one battery of rifled Whitworth guns.

H1: Soldier, *Brigata Dunne*

The British volunteers were dressed in white; note the green cuffs, and his red neckerchief obscuring a low-standing green collar. As an alternative to the kepi, a 'pillbox' cap in white or red might be worn. The weapon is an Enfield rifle.

H2: Soldier, *Compagnia Straniera*

This company of Swiss deserters was dressed in a simple but smart dark blue and blue-grey uniform, with red trim on the falling collar, shoulder straps, front, round cuffs, pocket flaps and trouser seams, and a red kepi. His weapon is the Federal Swiss M1851 rifle.

H3: Trooper, *Legione Ungherese*

While the Hungarian cavalry squadron's dark blue uniform with red hussar lace and cording is unsurprising apart from the unusual peaked cap with a falling red bag, it is more curious that the company of infantry wore a very similar uniform – see MAA 512, Plate D2.

H4: Officer, *Guide a Cavallo*

During the campaign of 1860 the Mounted Guides used two different hussar-style uniforms; until the fall of Palermo they wore the one represented here, which was then replaced by a new kepi, dolman and trousers in grey, with black trim and gold sleeve knots.

Officer of Garibaldi's Mounted Guides wearing the unit's second uniform (compare with Plate H4). Colours: grey kepi with gold triple rank lace and buglehorn; grey dolman with black frogging, piping and trefoil shoulder cords; gold Hungarian sleeve knots, and gold-embroidered pouch belt; grey trousers with black double side-stripes; black sword knot. (Courtesy Anne S.K. Brown Military Collection, Brown University Library, Providence RI)

INDEX